Di Bag

CW01403441

ARRIVAL PRESS

DISTANT MEMORIES

Edited

By

TIM SHARP

First published in Great Britain in 1997 by
ARRIVAL PRESS
1 - 2 Wainman Road, Woodston,
Peterborough, PE2 7BU

All Rights Reserved

Copyright Contributors 1996

HB ISBN 1 85786 511 1
SB ISBN 1 85786 506 5

Foreword

Is your last holiday just a distant memory, with only a few photos to remind you of those lazy relaxing days when you didn't give the usual daily grind so much as a thought?

This collection of verse contains the holiday memories of the authors, whether happy or sad, romantic memories or just recalling far away islands.

However you spent your last holiday I am sure that after reading this collection you'll feel relaxed and the memories will return, or you'll be thumbing through the new brochures and making plans for that next trip away from it all.

Tim Sharp
Editor

CONTENTS

ROLL ON SUMMER

Summer now has gone
Autumn hurries in
Night is falling fast
Long social gatherings
Now in the past

Hot lazy days
Spent on the beach
Holidays in foreign lands
And exotic countries
Far out of reach

Back to reality
Our normal life
With memories galore
Of sand, sea and sun
To rejuvenate the spirit
Till summer comes once more.

Elizabeth Amery

TRAVELLERS' TALES

Thinking back to all the holidays, and places I have been,
I remember so many wonderful things, and glorious sights I've seen.
Travelling round the world to famous cities, and tiny villages too,
From ancient Roman towns like Pompeii, to sights both strange and new.
I've sailed across the Channel, flown through the sky for hours,
Stood on snowy mountain tops, and in alpine valleys full of flowers.
Visited West Virginia in the Fall, gazed at the Southern Cross on high,
In unpolluted New Zealand, where stars seem to fill the sky.
Explored fantastic eastern temples, the canals in Amsterdam,
Been up Toronto's C N Tower, the tallest built by man!
Walked down the Mall in Washington, the one in London too,
Gazed at jewels in the Tower, and lakes of deepest blue.
In quiet, peaceful valleys, colourful flowers at my feet,
Seen exotic birds and plants in Hawaii, tried new kinds of food to eat!
Rowed in a gondola in Venice, haggled in bazaars,
Hoping to get a bargain. Walked tracks untouched by cars.
Been to the opera in Vienna, walked through Black Forest trees,
Tramped up glaciers in Switzerland - I thought my toes would freeze!
Had morning coffee in 'Raffles' in Singapore, and in the Yorkshire Dales,
Motor-cycled through lovely countryside, in Scotland and in Wales.
I've stayed in top hotels, and bed and breakfasts, done some camping too,
And hopefully, in years to come, there will be lots more to do!
Though I'm just an ordinary lass, I'm lucky, I'll agree,
To have been able to do so many things, to keep in my memory.

Kathleen Adams

A MEMORY A MOMENT

How lovely when you have a moment
Think back to your last holiday
Looking through things you now treasure
And dreaming of boats in the bay
All with the purest white sails
The sea just as blue as the sky
With me and a handsome tanned male
On a towel we lay side by side
Thinking of strolls in the moonlight
The kisses we shared moments gone
And the sadness I felt when we parted
At the airport before coming home
But then as I look through his letters
Declaring his undying love
A red rose he lovingly gave me
Pressed in my small book of verse
A wonderful memory, a moment
Remembered with more than a sigh
For a holiday long to be cherished
As I lay all my treasures aside

Jeanette Gaffney

SPANISH HILLS

Donkey trekking in yonder hills was lots of fun.

There were tales of a rogue donkey
In the pack and you can guess
Who was on his back, me of course.

The trek goes through sandy hills,
Then all at once my donkey runs away,
And I have lost control,
To the top of a hill he runs
Leaving our group behind.

The donkey returns to our group
Showing me that he is well trained
And in full control.

Everyone has a good laugh
And we all move off
On our trek across the countryside
Having lots of fun.

Gerald Snook

MEMORIES

I still hear the gentle waves
Breaking on the shore
My heart skips and misses a beat
To be with you again once more

To feel the sand beneath my feet
Would make my dreams come true
How I wish that I could be
Back on that beach with you

Those sunny days and balmy nights
Will never leave my mind
Nor the tears of sadness
When I left you behind

You said to me 'I love you'
In your special Spanish way
'Recuerdo' means 'memories'
Till we meet again one day.

Toni-Marie Benton

THAT COTTAGE

Strolling down a leafy lane,
Thatched cottage I espied.
Could not erase it from my mind,
No matter how I tried.

Something from the past it stirred,
Deep in my memory.
Then, suddenly I remembered,
A long forgotten holiday.

Funny how little things,
Can make the mind awake.
How happy we were playing there,
At the cottage by the lake.

Only seems like yesterday,
Yes it's fifty years or more.
On our last family holiday,
Before Dad went to war.

G W Bailey

MEMORIES OF PARADISE

Unpacking my suitcase, I found some sand,
It reminded me of distant lands,
Sunny weather, palm trees,
Sparkling blue sea, warm beach,
I can't forget the happy time I had,
Over the last few weeks in the Med,
Working on my tan, feeling at ease,
Walking along in the evening breeze,
Now I'm back home again, nothing seems the same,
I'll have to get back into this way of life again,
But I'll be saving like made just you wait and see,
Memories of paradise will be a reality for me.

Claire Young

I'M MOTORING ON MY HOLIDAYS

I'm motoring on my holidays, I can't believe it's true.
If you hadn't been away for five years you would feel the same way too.
I'm tired of cooking and cleaning every single day.
I can't believe after all this time, I'm finally getting away.
Poor mothers have it hard, you know, they don't work from nine till five.
Sometimes at the end of the day I don't know if I'm dead or alive.
There's all these endless tasks to do every minute of the day.
Eee! I still can't believe I'm going away!
I really must try to wipe all these things from my mind.
No happier woman than me could you ever wish to find.
I'm looking forward very much to my well deserved rest.
Thank the Lord, on this day I really do feel blessed.
I'm motoring on my holidays, I can't believe it's true.
I'm trying to take it in, you know, even the sky looks a lovely blue,
I'm with my husband and my daughter and that makes it right.
I love my little girl, you know, to me she's a sheer delight.
The three of us are happy, motoring in our car,
We've prayed for travelling mercies because we're travelling far.
I'm just sitting here thinking how lucky I am.
All that planning and packing and our holidays finally began.
A full ten days, yes, that will do me.
There's plenty places and people I plan to see.
Looking up old friends, I love doing that.
To relax, have a cup of tea and a little chat.
I'm not a greedy person, I don't expect a lot.
In fact I've always been happy with what I've got.
Now I'm motoring on my holiday, I still can't believe it's true
I hope I'm not just dreaming because I'd be sad, wouldn't you?

Edith Meldrum Cooke

RELIVING HOLIDAYS AS A CHILD

When as a child the family went to Rhyl in a train.
Travelling those days you felt dirty and it was a strain
To Rhyl in North Wales was our destination.
For a holiday for a lovely week's holiday was our vocation.

My sister, brother and myself to the beach with spades and pails.
Making sandcastles and trenches and watching boats sail.
Driving our parents mad to go on the bikes
Going to the open air theatre and open air circus was my life.

M P Morrey

TENERIFE

It's Tuesday morning I'm sitting on the bed
God sits beside me shaking his head
As he listens to me talking to myself
Wondering how to begin my day
The night before all was not well
Thoughts within me, all I could tell

In Tenerife away from home
Hot hot sun, all I did was roam
Looking for answers, where was I going
God tells me to listen and stop the moaning
Measuring time with cigarettes I've smoked
Coffee, tea, bathing suits soaked.

Don't project it's a brand new day
Get off that bed and be on your way
Make the most of the negative feeling
Start the day right and stop your head reeling
Wake up your daughter, although she's not well
Today will be different, try it then tell

You don't need money to have a good time
Just be happy, things will be fine
God I know all these things
I just miss my mother
Not long since she died
Just seems further and further

What can I do show me the way
Keep me right, just for this day
I know I'm asking but am I listening
I really will try, keep on insisting
God replies, enough of this stuff
Come on Jean, you asked life's tough . . .

Jean Tennent Mitchell

THE VISIT

We went to the sea and the golden sands,
We ate loads of ice cream each day.
We took Brutus for walks through the woods and the fields,
And made nests in the sweet smelling hay.

We saw a fine show of dancing on ice,
And perched on the edge of our seats.
We also went shopping for footballs and spacemen,
Pyjamas and jerseys and treats!

We chased round the garden and played hide and seek.
We only had one stressful day -
When the tortoise got out, but thanks to Sharp Eyes
She didn't walk too far away.

We read stories at night and we laughed and we sang.
We found butterflies, scarlet and blue.
On the last day I asked them what they had liked best.
And they said, 'Being here Gran with you!'

Anne Marie Bowles

DISTANT MEMORIES

A dream come true, passports correct, visas too, cases are
packed, we are on our way.
The plane starts to move, the magic begins, we feel as if it
Were the 'wind beneath our wings'.
Faraway places become real to us, Muscat, Singapore, Sydney.
Not for us the Opera House or Sydney Bridge, famous tho'
they be.
First it is friends, then birds the flowers, the space the
Sun, the sparkling sea.
The gardens where Frangipani, Hibiscus, and Fiddle Woods bloom
Bananas for breakfast - go pick your own.
Are we really so far from home, yes, they really are dolphins
At play just beyond the surging foam.
To hold silver ore, Amethyst, treasure from the earth,
Seashells that were once someone's home, for us far
Beyond any monetary worth.
To wake with the dawn to hear the hoot of the train on its
one per daily run.
Pure enjoyment each day, thanks to our friends, we wished
Our holiday would never end.
The distance is only in time, the memories are still as clear
As if it were yesterday.

D Willans

A STROLL THROUGH ST ANDREWS

On the cobbled paves of Market Street
We browsed among the shops.
With our holiday home at the Cathedral end,
We made infrequent stops.
Too tempting were the sights and sounds
Of Old St Andrews town
As we searched amid the bric-a-brac
Of the stalls that showed their wares.
We found the best in bread and cakes
And the butcher's mince was great!
A sweet shop tucked just near the Wynd
Was a treasure chest to find.
We had lots to do and did it all
With memories, such fun.
The city tour on open bus
Took in the sights on a breezy run.
The witch walk with its friendly ghost
Acting as our host
Took us down dark and eerie lanes
And we screamed at phantoms for our gains!
After this the sea life beckoned
And with friends, Margaret and Stewart
A visit now was reckoned.
We saw fish and sharks, eels and seals
Sea horses, tiny and sweet.
But, truth to tell, hunger called
And it made us want to eat!
So, we found the 'Old Union' and ordered our brunch
But wasps thought of Margaret as breakfast and lunch!
Too fast the days passed, for Drew, Fern and me,
But, fear not St Andrews
We'll be back next year.

Moira Brabender

HOLIDAYS

The thoughts of holidays conjure up a sunset beach and a life of luxury
Although it's only going to be a week or two sheer heaven it's going to be
I think some years ago we took a break not just because we were bored
In fact to fly half round the world we just could not afford
Some people's idea of holiday is to drive almost until they drop
And although some of the family's not enjoying it the driver doesn't want
                                                                            to stop
It seems to me that for many life is lived at such a pace
That even pleasurable pursuits that they seek are almost like a race
A holiday surely should give one the opportunity to relax
But it seems when you get to the chosen venue you could be ready to
                                                                            collapse
You spend some time getting to the airport and checking out your flight
But you find it's delayed so you wait in the lounge sometimes into the night
At last you're called that all is well and you're at least on your way
Beginning to get frustrated because like other passengers you've almost
                                                                            lost a day
But of the one or two whose holidays end up with disaster
Many thousands enjoy it all - a sort of memories ever after
Some people go on holiday when things go wrong and to get away from life
But life is what we make it and the break won't help if there is strife
If you're content with someone your life is more or less complete
You do not need exotic holidays in order to compete
If you have some time away it's not to improve your lot
It will be just an extension of what you've already got
So before you take your holiday get reasons right, it needn't be too grand
In fact with children in particular all they may want most is just a
                                                                            square of sand

Reg Morris

HOLIDAY ROMANCE

It all began one holiday along the prom at Whitley Bay,
We met, we smiled and said hello, how do you do, you looked so sweet and
charming too,
(You looked so smart and handsome too)
Soon hand in hand we strolled along with the crowd on the prom,
Just a girl and just a boy full of love and full of joy
And our love was so strong nothing seemed could go wrong
But, life has its ups and downs, even kings can lose their crowns,
I lost your love when you went away at the end of that holiday,
If only we could go back in time to those golden days when you were mine
But Father Time always has his way we can never return to yesterday
But, deep within my heart and memory,
You will always be a part of me.

H R Coupe

15

NORWAY IN SEPTEMBER

A sheet of water, clear and still
Reflecting every tree and hill
Fresh air with just a touch of chill
That's Norway in September.

Mountain slopes clad with trees
Moving gently in the breeze
Autumn colours on the leaves
That's Norway in September.

The waterfalls drop from great height
The water rushing foaming white
While rainbow colours sparkle bright
In the sunshine of September.

I'd like to live for evermore
In a little house upon the shore
Of a fjord. Who could ask for more
I love Norway in September.

Elizabeth Cook

16

TRAVELLING LIGHT

I usually travel for a change and a rest;
The taxi takes the change and the hotel takes the rest!

Kimbo

SONNET ON PARIS

Graceful is the city we call Paris!
Golden figures guard the 'Palais de Chaillot',
Terraced houses edge the 'Isle de St Louis'.
Royal treasures fill the Palace of La Louvre;
From eerie lights around the 'Mona Lisa'
To Grecian urns, Etruscon comedy, below . . .
White domes grace the Sacre Coeur Basilica
And everywhere, arches, statues, flashing fountains, flow.
Amidst the greenery, march, a multitude of trees
That with the Tuileries give serenity, and space,
That cut the traffic fumes and dim the noise
Of modern transportation! Slower is the pace
Than London town. Female girls, sprucer boys;
Smart kindly folk - unafraid to chatter.
That saucy world is held within Monmatre?

Sylvia M Dixon Ward

THE HOLIDAY WE'LL NEVER FORGET

Now our holidays are over, and back to work are we
We ponder on those brochures that told us what to see
They painted such a picture of sand and sun and sea
But was it all like that in harsh reality,
We started off at crack of dawn, kids gave me quite a head
Car broke down on motorway, petrol in the red
The air was blue as it could be, won't tell you what I said
The flight was just too awful after a very long delay
The food not any better I heard folk round me say
We thought well this is it, it surely can't get worse
But before we got to our hotel I had to call a nurse
You may think that's the end of story, you would be very wrong
We won't be going there again, 'cause we couldn't stand the pong!

Vera Hobbs

DESTINATION: BLACKPOOL

Our destination is beautiful Blackpool,
can't wait to get there, can you?
I'm grown up, but yet act as a child,
because holidays make me so wild.
There is no sun, but the illuminations,
which can make a memorable vacation,
I visit the Pleasure Beach and have fun,
just until I experience the 'Big One'!
I'm travelling up real slow, then *Bop!*
I'm zooming right down to a sheer drop,
twisting, turning, zooming around,
I'm breathless and hear no sound,
apart from my heart in my throat,
the adrenaline so high I could choke.
At last! I am back to my earth,
So very thankful I'm not hurt.
I am waiting til' I could go again,
to Blackpool, the lights and the adrenaline.
Yes, this truly made my holiday,
Blackpool memories will never fade away.

Kim Ashcroft

SPANISH STRANGER

The holiday is over,
I'm on my way home,
Back to reality once again,
I'll always remember his face,
The tan and gleaming smile,
The first night there I began to stare,
And wished for something to happen,
I saw him first in the cafe where we ate,
He cooked my evening meal,
He wore his chef whites with pride,
I glanced now and then,
And smiled a shy smile,
My heart skipped a beat when he noticed,
Staring as he worked,
The language barrier was a problem,
I was too nervous to try,
Until the last day he decided to speak,
His English wasn't too good,
His eyes smiled as he spoke,
He seemed to show great interest,
I said my goodbye with a lingering kiss,
And touch of the hand,
Then I saw his wedding band,
My heart was shattered,
Thoughts of what could have been,
If it wasn't for the distance, language
                        or his wedding vows!

Kerry Firman

GOOD TIMES

Good times remembered from days of the past
The flowers of the spring the greenness of grass
The smile of a child, to the birth of a babe
A place in the sun, or children at play

Life as we know a difficult phase
Count all your blessings as you stand on life's stage
Hoping for peace and yet there are wars
Tempting us ever to settle old scores

So remember the good times it's stillness and peace
And pray that our World true and lasting Peace
For the good times so rare, precious as gold
And times to remember when we are old.

Patricia Thoirs

22

SEASON'S END

Recently vast crowds gathered here
Sunsoaking on the soft gold sand,
Splashing amidst such gentle waves,
A toddler holding tight to a parent's hand.

Millions flocking to a sun-washed beach
Filling warm air with shouts of delight,
Vast castles built upon the sand
And joyful children flying coloured kites.

By night the town is a glittering strand
Of brightly lit cafés, discos and bars
With music throbbing through the hours,
Echoing to a crystal cover of stars.

Now a still stretch of fine-grained sand
Watched by shuttered and silent eyes
Of hotels thronging along the shoreline,
Only witnesses to a lonely bird's cries.

Most places silent and strangely forlorn,
Just empty regiments of tables and chairs,
One day a café the next a still space
While quietness stalks streets and squares.

Sun umbrellas lie wrapped and stacked,
High season thundered at a mighty pace
Running so fast for such a short time,
Before succumbing to winter's embrace.

Season's end and most have turned home,
Priceless land sweeping to sky each way
Echoing only to the sounds of the sea,
Already a million footprints swept away.

Elizabeth Lucas

HOLIDAY FEELINGS

Cases packed, last minute checks,
Don't want no cock-ups, or regrets.
Taxi's here, we're on our way,
This is it - *our holiday.*

Morning sun, now turning hot,
Throats parched, no coffee pot,
Coach arrives, on board we go,
Heading for the sea - you know.

Three hours later, and we're there,
Cases on the pavement stare,
Off we truggle to find some digs,
Hot and weary, all of a *tis!*

'Vacancies' there are - *everywhere.*
But what's it like inside there?
We take a chance and in we go,
Relieved at last - does it really show?

Settled in, and now relaxed,
Off we go to have a few laughs,
A wander round to see *what's on,*
A cup of coffee, a buttered scone.

The dinner gong sounds out its boom,
We make our way to the dining room,
Friendly faces there to meet,
We get tucked in to a real treat.

Well fed, and contented, on day one,
We take the night air along the prom,
Then it's off for a shower, and into bed,
Refreshed, and clean for the day ahead.

Michael John Swain

ANTIQUITIES

On Capri's high and mighty shore the Emperor Tiberius
A lofty palace once decreed and our intent was serious
To climb the cliff and scale his walls, although the way might weary us.

The path was steep, the sun was hot upon that rugged Isle
With heavy tread we'd plodded out the last and longest mile
And staggered to the entrance gate with tired, but gallant, smile.

This sprightly white-haired lady whispered charmingly to me
'Just show the man your Pension book and you can get in free.'
She couldn't tell, God bless her, but we're barely fifty three!

Lin Sarjeant

HOLIDAY PARADISE

Sandy beaches on a tropical island,
Sun and sea and laughter,
Perfect skies of deepest blue,
Last for ever after,
Trickling rain in waterfalls,
Breezes blowing by,
Whispering winds and rustling trees,
Birds flying free in the sky,
Moonlit nights and twinkling stars,
Sunsets reflect in the haze,
Darkness falls and closes its eyes,
On another of summer's best days.

Carolyn Finch

MEMORIES OF BRITTANY

Old granite walls, mellowed by sun
Butterflies, buddleia and bumbling bees' hum.
Shimmering lunches of cheese and cold wine
Cascading geraniums, warm grapes on the vine.
Tight shuttered windows seeming asleep
Tantalising glimpses through doorways so deep.
Shadowy churches, cool, lofty and bare.
Pinpricked with candles, lit with such care.
Three circling buzzards, in sky of pure blue,
Calling and calling in wild piercing mew.
Cows and corn and Muscadet
Frantic tractors baling hay.
The colours of Brittany, blue, red and white
On sailing boats, shutters and fountains of light.
Blue black is the sky so deep in the night,
Sprinkled with stars and Milky Way bright.
The sound of the silence deafens the ear,
Broken by owl call, wondrously near.

Though summer has flown, I will not forget
Or think of past days, tinged with regret
But recall all the laughter and soft morning haze
And recapture it all in the cold winter days.

Valerie Coleman

MAJORCAN MEMORIES

Sun, sand and sea; not everyone's cup of tea
but I love the sun, and being by the sea.
I'm lucky to have a flat by it, where?
Well, a place a couple of hours away, by air.

Majorca, by some much maligned
by reputation of *package* only assigned,
to burgers and chips, discos and booze
where hooligans play all night and daily snooze.

Some rowdy resorts do exist, it's true
but there is so much more to do;
take a drive up mountains covered in pines,
valleys growing oranges, lemons and vines.

My little flat, comfortable, colourful but only small,
a quarter century's memories within the walls.
A balcony upon which to sit and view
sea, sky, sunrise and evening hues.

Where for less than a fiver, I eat my lunch
in a café below with friends, a very mixed bunch,
The 'Menu del Dia' includes bread and vino
So, we eat, drink, talk in many a lingo.

Perhaps later in the day we plan a 'fiesta'
but not until we've parted, for a siesta.
Days idle along, some shopping, some chores,
A swim, or a walk along the shores.

Then, Adios! My little island, it's back to the other
Until 'Ola! Again, for you my senses to recover.
Back to work, money to save and earn
So that I can to your warmth return.

Jane Uff

SEASIDE HOLIDAY

We found our Island in the sun
For relaxation by the sea
Surrendering to the blessing of
The joy of being free.

The sea birds called, the air was cool
Before the heat of day
As we went forth to greet the dawn
Bracing, beside the bay.

Then lazing by the ocean blue
Upon soft golden sands
Once more to feel their warmth
Go sifting through our hands.

Lastly, to take a stroll along
The shore, when day was done
As in the glow of evening
We watched the setting sun.

A swim, a walk, a suntan,
A feeling of God's grace.
For when you are beside the sea
The world falls into place.

Joan Heybourn

SUMMER HOLIDAY

A couple of months on, I look back,
Did I really do all that,
Packed my case, off I flew,
To a place I never knew,
Land at airport, taken to the hotel,
The language I did, not know too well,
Once I unpacked, had a look to see,
What was in and around me,
Took a taxi, went to a bar,
Stayed fairly central, didn't go far,
A good look to see, what I could find,
Had several places here in mind,
Took a train to see the view
Seeing this country, I never knew,
Rivers and mountains, and all the scenery,
Colourful, picturesque, full of beauty,
Went on the chair lift, what a thrill,
I travelled higher, than the hills,
Horse riding, trekking, did the lot,
A busy day, was what I got,
Dancing, every evening long,
Full of energy, kept going strong,
Swimming was the best for me,
In the pool I love to be,
But it had to come to an end,
All my day I did spend,
I did so much, this holiday the best,
I felt I came home for a rest,
Memories here, will always be,
I may go back again, we'll see.

Lynn Hallifax

MY CHILDHOOD TRIP

Once a year I always looked forward to my trip upon a train.
With my worried face pressed against the window asking is it going to rain
We walked happily down Cowbridge Road to Ely's crowded railway station
Written on a large board Barry Island was our destination.

We climbed aboard that coal-fired smoke-covered train
The excitement was so great as it filled my heart and entered my brain
I will always remember that sweet moment we all shouted we had arrived
there
To see the crowded beach filled with those candy stripped chairs.

With my shiny new bucket and spade held tightly in my hands
When we spent those sun-filled hours running so free across the sands.
With our childhood voice we would shout with happy screams.
Our faces were covered with streams of melted chocolate ice-cream.

Then we gathered around the shop that sold those fish and chips.
When Barry Island's colourful stores showed those wooden ships.
We will always recall our childhood outing to the seaside crowded fair
The evening breeze was so strong as it sweetly tossed our sand-filled hair.

Our summer day outing swiftly ended, as we walked slowly back to
Barry's station
We all knew that Ely children's home was sadly our homeward destination
With great sadness in our hearts I knew we would arrive home late
I will always remember my carefree day as we walked thro' those iron gates.

John Frederick Grainger

HOLIDAYS

Having travelled far and near
There's always one thing I hold dear
That's after being away for a few days or more
To come back home, and open my front door.
Oh it's lovely to travel and see the world
And different sites as they unfurl
To look at cultures and wonderful scenes
And all the other bits and in-betweens.
To meet people, make friends anew
This is all about holidays and what you do
Then when you come to look at your snaps
And realise a certain time now, has to elapse
Before you venture again next year
And then that dreaded packing comes near
That's the worst of your vacation
Looking for your case at whatever station
Or the frustration of that carousel
Looking for your case there as well
Next is that trolley, is there one around?
You grab it quick if there's one to be found
And now you say 'Home for a decent cup of tea'
That will suit you and definitely me.

Jean Linney

YOUR TOWN . . . ISRAEL

I want to scream and make loud noises,
I want to shout and jump about.
For I see only troubled faces,
when I go walking around your town.

I see the girl with the baby.
I see a beggar who is blind.
I see a man without his family,
walking the city grounds.

I look for solutions and do not find them.
I looked for equality and could not see it.
I looked for happiness in people' s faces,
whilst visiting your town.

I found bitterness and sorrow, tied together with love.
I found confusion and harmony, within your people's hearts.
I found God and Jesus, loving all nations.
When I took time and listened,
to your town.

H M Sweeney

CRUISING DOWN TO THE CANARIES

My wife and I, went on a *fly-cruise*
To that Italian ship, that was sailing from Genoa,
On the plane, my wife pointed, and said 'Look, isn't that Mary White?
So I looked - Mary White, Mary White? No - I don't know her.

Later that day, we boarded the 'Enrico Costa'
Greeted at the gangway by officers wearing gold braid,
We found our cabin - it was OK - but difficult for *swinging cats*
For a moment - I regretted the money, that I had paid.

Our first port of call was *Cadiz*
It looked like a typical Spanish town,
They served a nice cold lager, if you drink *lager*
But - when I asked for a *Brown* - there came a frown.

Then, off we sailed to the *Canaries*
Las Palmas - *Gomez* and *Tenerife,*
Probably, a peaceful spot, out of season
But in August, it was Bank Holiday on Hampstead Heath.

Now we were really enjoying our *cruise*
With a good suntan - the ship's pool and tempting food,
But, when it came to wearing a Louis XIV wig, for *fancy dress night*
I said 'No,' I wasn't in that kind of mood.

Our last port of call was *Gibralter*
Still *British* - but - most shopkeepers weren't
Decided to have a meal on dry land
Our *coffee* was tepid, and the toast was burnt.

The last night's *gala* on the ship was excellent
Next day, we flew back home,
Where my wife whispered laughingly, in my ear
Those *Italian officers* were so handsome
Maybe next time - I ought to go *alone.*

Paul Gold

MAGIC MOMENTS

Majorca, Minorca, Naples and Rome,
What wonderful sights.
And they say 'There's no place like home!'

Dusseldorf, Cologne, 'Die Lorelei' on the Rhine;
Heidelberg - where 'the Student Prince' had a good time.

Brussels and Paris - Napoleon's tomb;
Lakes, museums and art in spacious Stockholm.

Portafino, Mount Vesuvius and ruined Pompeii;
- then a boat trip to see Gracie Fields on Capri.

Lake Garda, Verona - home of Shakespeare's
great theme
Of tragic young lovers lost in their dream.

Nice, Cannes and Monaco to see Princess Grace,
From a holiday village, where this all took place.

The Austrian Alps and the Lake of Lucerne,
Bavaria, The Black Forest - new visions to learn.

On the Costa Brava, Spanish ladies in their black dress,
In Germany, old men in the parks, playing with chess.

Dubrovnik - with icons so brilliant a display
Of their Christian faith held for many a day.

What wonders, what glories that I have seen
On my trips abroad, over the years there have been;
Give me a ticket - yes, I've got the bug,
Travelling's my wicket - not home on a *rug*.

Beatrice Wilson

SCARBOROUGH FAIR

The rolling swell of sea, makes grief
As fleeing bathers seek relief,
In bay front taverns they sit adjourned
To Scarborough town, I had returned.

This flower set in Yorkshire Dales,
Resplendent in its hills and vales,
It's castle walls defending *nowt*,
Unable to keep the tourists out.

The harbour bustles beneath its tor,
As fishermen reel their catch ashore,
Along the dock do dories snuggle,
All plump with herring, cod and mackerel.

Upon the streets an endless melee
Of people passing their time away,
The promenade offers no sun dodgers shade
From 'Peasholme Park to South Parade'.

Sea front hill trams' engines pound
With funicular passengers townward bound,
Surveying down from its dizzying height
A spectacular display of lights at night.

Peace and serenity falls silently deep
As I drift away to a restful sleep,
My body immersed with fresh coastal air
In Bronte Country, in Scarborough Fair.

Michael Gardner

A VIEW OF THE PACIFIC OCEAN

Breakfast time in swiftest motion:
Below white waves on vast green ocean.
A sea bird's view; but from a height
To which no sea bird soars. No land in sight.

Folk from three lands look down upon
The mighty sea. See no ships thereon.
Three lands, three nations, but one speech.
The islands of the south to reach.

Folk from the isles of the far north
Come to the isles of the far south
Their beauty and their art to see,
and meet with kin a world apart; maybe.

Folks of the isles of the far south
Homeward from isles of the far north;
Land from which forebears came, to see;
And meet with kin a world apart, maybe.

To make our journey fast and good;
See all is well and bring us food.
Folk of that mighty northern land.
(But that airline had to disband).

Brown cliffs come quickly: New Zealand
End of journey from old England.
Nine thirty, this Saturday morning.
What cousins for us the barrier adorning?

Frances Joan Tucker

'SCENTS' OF SMELL

What's happened to all the childhood smells?
I ask in consternation.
Exciting, smoky, sulphury, smells,
Of Liverpool Street Station.

We'd board the musty, dusty, train,
Our journey had begun.
For it was holiday time again,
We craved the sea and sun.

Great Yarmouth, with its salty smells
Of pitch and tar and oakum,
Great ships, berthed all along the quay,
The spices, wood, the hokum.

The curing sheds, along the wharf,
The smell of oak chips burning,
The rows of herring hanging there,
Soon kippers, for the turning.

The sickly sweet, and peppermint smell
Of lettered rock, from rock shops swelled.
The bags of fruit, sold on the beach,
The scented pear, the fragrant peach.

The yeasty smells from country inns,
The lavender fields, the biscuit tins.
The sweet peas, sold to passing coaches,
All remembered, as old age encroaches.

What's happened to them all I wonder?
Should like to know, afore I go under.
If you can tell me, please do tell.
Or have I lost my sense of smell?

Hilda Jones

NIAGARA

I hear the thunder of the falls - then I see that great cataract
As it calls, the great white rapids falling
Over that great horseshoe edge.
Floating, dreaming, through misty waters,
Hearing the thunder from above,
As the waters fall on rocks below,
Bouncing off as a misty cloud.
I float and dream with her - this spirit of the waterfall,
Walking through waters clear,
Disappearing into the mist.
She guards these falls without fear.
I feel the water on my body - yet no force to do ill,
Only her spirit that walks with me.
I feel her gentle kiss upon my cheek,
Her force blows the wind as a gentle breeze
Making leaves move gently on the trees.
She is calm, yet she gives her strength,
To save some souls from these great falls,
As the spirit of the water she will call
As she calls me - to write these words,
Leylawala, Maid of the Mist, we will remember - she guards these falls
To help save all those who are called
To challenge this great thundering waterfall,
Her waterfall of tears are shed in sorrow
For those she cannot save.
As the great white misty waters rise as a tower
It reaches out to places beyond our power.
Our lives, like rapids, can be full of troubles,
Let us not forget, like this wondrous waterfall,
Life can also hold, beauty, laughter, and divine love.

Mary Wright

WINDSWEPT MEMORIES

It's on nights like this
As the wind blows cold,
And strips the trees of autumn gold;
That the sound of the sea
Swells in my ear,
And reminds me of the shore this year.

It was a break of some days that flew right by,
As we trudged over cliffs to where the gulls fly,
And gazed on waters, foamy white,
With mist and spray obscuring sight.
And against the purple blue of falling night,
We saw the lighthouse pumping light,
And walked the dog on crackling stone,
And on barren dunes we let it roam.

But still I remember that desolate bay,
Where no-one stirred to, night or day,
Where we gathered shells
And bleached dry wood,
Dragging trails to where we stood.

Those days are gone now,
Though we clutch to them like the sands
That are scattered on those shorelines,
Time runs steadily through our hands.

Emma J Christmas

WHEN YOUR WORK IS DONE

Blue painted skies, fading overhead
Looking down at the beach
Sand coloured red
Seas all aglow from the moon that's above
Lights of the town
Flickering with love
Red, green and orange
Shine down from the wall
Buildings so proud
Stand aloft,
Standing tall.
Headlands pulled out from the wet form a cove
For the land, sea and sky
To meet on that road
Trees have stood still
From time since begun
Sapping the energy of life
From the sun
But those blue painted skies now faded overhead
Are covered by cloud
That's best left unsaid
They can't spoil the choice or hinder the fun
In a place just like this
When your work is done

Steve Randell

UNTITLED

Didn't we have a lovely time
The day we went to Bowness
The M61 and then the M6
Soon we were in Cumbria
Along country lanes and down leafy dales
We never gave up laughing
Until we arrived at a wonderful site
And the wheels went round.

There was Tony and Sue and Wendy and Geoff
And David with his Sheila
Mary and George and Sylvia and Keith
And Sheila with her Tony.
We had burgers and buns, and sausages too
And then we had some wino
Our neighbours peeped out from behind
Their closed blinds
And the word went round.

We were all up at ten for coffee
And then, we had a funny raffle
Our Wendy was pleased with a packet of 3s
And Tony won yesterday's paper
And Geoff was surprised when he won the
Last prize
Of yesterday's left-over barbie
We said our farewells to the sound
Of church bells
Then our wheels went round.

Mary Childs

SUMMERTIME ON BREDON

Green hillocks
White cumulus
Blue patches of sky
Cool water
Geese flying calling
Weathered cottages
Undulating landscape
Sheep chewing staring
Summertime on Bredon

Margaret Bennett

THE CRUISE THAT NEVER WAS

We were packed and ready for our cruise,
When in the post arrived the news.
The ship would not be setting sail,
Her engines had begun to fail.
Two weeks in a hotel instead
The very thought filled me with dread.

But when we arrived and looked around,
No fault at all could be found.
We met some folk from Essex way
And all together we enjoyed our stay
Our friendship still is going strong.
So maybe fate made things go wrong.

We drank lots of wine, laid in the sun,
Swam in the pool, had loads of fun.
So now I feel I must confess,
What seemed a tragedy, turned into success.

Valerie Green

SEASIDE THROUGH CITY EYES

Computer-generated ocean.
Press the buttons on my rock-chisled remote control,
Change waves from turquoise to grey. Light to dark.
Fairground lights and ecstasy rides,
In solitude past ghost train water flumes.

Minute crab blags space between plastic shells, squats.
Polystyrene cartons float -
The new breed of man-made fish.

Bored of this film. Press the buttons.
Change cyber sky to rain,
Will wash the half-dressed families away,
When too hot too cold, they complain,
Or stay home within sanitised sanity,
So I turn the dial on my rock right down.

Waltzers twist to rave tunes,
I, clubland mutation, am coming down,
Adapted an equilibrium with inner-city madness -
Yet on these hard shingles, all and only ocean in sight,
There is space to confront savage, tangled truths. Harsh.

Small-town silence. Vastness of the sea is strange.
Toes venture nuclear waters,
Huge techno-gulls are moving cameras,
Their voice-overs screech above a sub-base of irrepressible tide.
No-one is here. I call back. Sing.
Salt-wind carries amplified particles, city dust.
Alone, I am the star of this video.

Michelle Blower

MEMORIES OF MY ETHIOPIAN HOLIDAY

Five weeks' holiday in Ethiopia spent with my son,
Proved to be a wonderful and exciting one.
Eight thousand feet up on beautiful terrain,
Like the Scottish Highlands without the rain.
There was no language problem since it is the rule
For English to be taught to children in school.
Addis Ababa itself had a communist stance,
Lenin's statue, sloganned archways, one saw at a glance.
Haile Selassie Parliament, glass panels portraying life
In Africa before communist onslaught and strife.
Emperor Menelik's abode, his regalia on display,
Jewelled robes and three-tiered crown in splendid array.
Staying overnight at Rift Valley Game Park where I saw,
Many rare animals, baboons and exotic birds galore.
At the British Embassy the private apartments I viewed,
Served with afternoon tea, my spirits renewed
Attending their party celebrating Armistice Day,
In a wonderful garden bright with floral display.
Visiting my son's fields of tef, the national grain,
Improving crops to prevent future famine again.
At all the modern hotels I was royally entertained,
The Hilton was by far the best, quite justly famed.
I learned the coffee bean we take for granted,
Originated in Ethiopia before being overseas planted
Visiting a famous leprosy hospital where patients learn,
To spin, weave and embroider a living to earn.
Seeing the statue of St George on main thoroughfare,
Strange to think with Ethiopia our patron saint we share.
Old churches with painted murals, distinctive and rare,
Depicting Biblical scenes, guarded with fanatical care.

E Kathleen Jones

WELL I SAID I NEEDED A REST

The summer had been changeable
But we hadn't had much rain
So we packed the motor caravan
For a week on a field in Kent

We arrived in September sunshine
And got ourselves settled in
The spot was most congenial
And then came down the rain

The dog lay in her basket
And the budgies were not impressed
We donned the fire and rugs around our legs
Then gave up and went to bed

The local radio played good music
And we sat and sang along
Nipped out between the showers
To walk the poor long-suffering dog

The crossword book was filled now
And the week drew to a close
This holiday was restful
So now can we please go home?

Markina

QUIET WATERS

Quiet waters, ducks and drakes
This is all it really takes
To slow one down from modern life
So full of noise and daily strife.

Quiet waters, hum of bees
In the clover, 'neath the trees
Along the bank grow poppies red
And one large daisy waves its head.

Quiet waters, gliding swan
The weary eye can rest upon
To store away within the soul
This vision that can make one whole.

Quiet waters, gentle breeze
Whisp'ring through the willow trees
Joins the birdsong harmony
Creating nature's symphony.

Quiet waters, sights and sounds
Ensure one's heart with joy abounds
When even back amidst the toil
Nothing can this memory spoil.

Barbara Lovering

A HOLIDAY AFLOAT

The soft slap of water on hull
And the gentle rocking of the boat
Herald a new day.

On deck, the early morning sun
Turns the mist to swirls of pink and gold,
And seagulls cry in their swooping, searching flight.

The boat rides easily to anchor
Breasting the tide,
And dark cliffs border the sandy bay.

On shore, shopkeepers open their doors
To early shoppers,
And dogs scamper on the tide-washed sands.

Below deck, the kettle sings on its gimballed stove
And soon the aroma of fresh coffee blends with the sea breeze.
The sizzle of bacon promises the satisfying of sea-born appetites.

Dishes washed and stacked away
And bunks neatly stowed -
Everything ship-shape below.

Up on deck, the sails snap and crackle,
The chain clatters as the anchor comes aboard,
And sheets are tightened round the winches.

Suddenly, the sails fill and billow
And a thrilling surge of power sends the boat forward.
Another glorious day at sea begins.

Sybil Mansell

A DESERT BIRTHDAY - MOROCCO 1993

Up at three on my birthday morning,
Of pleasures to come there was no warning.
In shorts of blue and shirt of red,
Teddy bear socks on feet of lead.
A wash in cold water, oh what a treat!
To ease the blisters of burning feet.
We bumped over sand that rattled our bones,
No light at all, no roadway cones.
The wagons they rattled and pitched in the dark
This was no gentle trip to a park.
We alighted at last and gazed at the sand,
We'd be climbing with Tuaregs hand within hand.
We struggled in sand right up to our knees
Oh God let me get to the top Oh please!
No word of English did my guide speak
But of last night's meal his breath did reek.
We reached the top going full throttle
Sipping together from my water bottle;
Cigarettes tasted stale as did the water
We sat together not 'guest' and 'porter'
He taught me my name in his native tongue
I'm glad that it's really not very long.
Coming down dunes was a lot faster
Soon I returned to being the 'master'
But I paid up his price without a thought
Contemplating the pleasures he'd brought.
The desert sunrise, the peace and the calm,
Climbing together going arm in arm.

Nina McKenna

HOLIDAYS REMEMBERED

Close your eyes and imagine cool drinks, the sun and the sand.
Listen and you'll hear waves as they lap close by to your hand.
Think of nights in the moonlight, strolling side by side,
Footprints left near the ocean disappearing with the tide.

The brilliance of a winter morn, snow reflecting the sun.
Walking through the whiteness until a slope invites the fun
Of running breathless in a race with no reason it would seem
Except to fall on the snow into the arms of a waking dream.

Imagination is freedom to drift along with thoughts,
A November day becomes August, the rain, a stream over rocks.
You are where and whom you wish, a memory through closed eyes
Which open to see reality and then the image dies.

Franklin H Smith

HOLIDAY ROMANCE

Barefoot along the sand,
The surf as bright as sunrise
And you beside me,
Lovely as the morning,
Your perfume took my breath.

The mist and salt scent rising
Blending to a memory,
A sweet fulfilment
Of last night's half-serious promise
To meet at dawn.

Surprising in its speed a reaching wave
Washing icy round our feet,
I swept you in my arms to lift you higher
Than the sly and cunning sea,
Shy blushing at the sudden closeness.

I should have kissed you then,
Your laughter broke the spell,
Unspoiled,
We were children playing in the surf.
Oblivious,

Sunning through the dayheat
Sharing one mind,
One understanding of our world,
Our chatter rehearsed, it seemed.
Came evening.

Still,
Warm.
The lowering sun filtered
Through green curtains.
The light was of the sea bed.

Michael Forrest

MY HOLIDAY TO IRELAND

I woke up bright and early
Got dressed and washed my face
I took my packed bag to the car
I had to make some space.

I got up to the airport
Where the planes fly low
I went into customs
My tickets were ready to show.

I flew over the Isle of Man
It really was quite fun
I went to Ireland with
My brother, dad and mum.

My Uncle Lawrence picked me up
At the other end
I hope there's loads of gift shops
I have ninety pounds to spend.

I met all my cousins
They were such great fun
Sometimes it just rained
Sometimes there was sun.

I stayed in a caravan
With my mum and dad
All the people over there
Are really really mad.

I went back to Belfast
It was my last day
There was trouble over there
I stayed out the way.

I got on the plane for home
Goodbye I did say
Thank you guys for everything.
I will be back some day.

Donna-Marie Scullion (13)

SYDNEY POSTE RESTANTE

Waiting in line - a questionable queue
of assorted world travellers, on a rainy afternoon.
All desperately hoping for a letter, for a clue,
that someone 10,000 miles away - someone remembers you.
The backpacker nightmare - the dread we all face,
is which direction from the computer's grinning screen you take.
Those who have friends, they're the lucky ones:
at the counter of collection backpacker kudos is won.
A dismal smile, disappointed shrug, of the one who turns away.
All eyes on you in pity, 'Sorry, no mail for you today.'
The shining ones: 'I've got a letter and you ain't,'
never spoken, but apparent, in Sydney Poste Restante.

Sarah C L Farmer

BURROWHAYES FARM

When holiday time comes around once more,
There's only one place to go, *Exmoor.*
To Burrowhayes Farm is the site that we go,
The welcoming hills and the people we know,
The horses, the woods, the stream running by,
Where Dunkery Hill seems to reach to the sky.

The mornings we spend in the stable to learn,
With brush or with bridle, we all have a turn.
The horses stand still, and tread with care.
None of them bite - only Domino would dare,
The blacksmith is coming, we might get a shoe.
We watch quiet and patiently, there's only a few.

Alyson and John take us out for an hour,
Maybe two, maybe four, regardless of shower,
They're out in the lead, to show us the way,
And bring us all back at the end of the day,
When the horses all trot up to the field to rest,
We think of our ride and decide it's the best.

The fancy dress ride is always fun,
This year a duo of tinkers won.
Mr 'D' comes to judge the grooming contest,
We've brushed and polished and hope our pony looks best,
To test everyone's skill, a horse quiz is planned,
Do you measure a horse by foot or by hand?

The days slip by, and our holiday ends,
Sadly, we must now say goodbye to our friends,
We've had happy days and memories to take home,
When on cold winter nights, our thoughts do roam
To the heather-clad hills and the valleys below,
The stream running by and the people we know.

Penny Dumelow

COACH TRIP

Sarnies packed, bottle of pop
Waiting for the coach to stop
Lady counts us, we're all here
We move off to a large cheer
Raffle tickets ten pence each
Hope it's something for the beach
Travelling really is such fun
Searching for the sea and sun
Had a go on all the rides
Held white-knuckled onto sides
Went up to the tower's very top
Thought the lift would never stop
Had a paddle, sea so cold
Can't complain, 'cos we were told
Game of Bingo, last to play
We've had such a lovely day
Time to find the coach car park
It's a good job it's not dark
Lady counts us, we're all here
Moving off, too tired to cheer
Fast asleep on the way back
Bought lots of rock, lost my mac
We're asked about trip next year
Try keeping us away my dear

Kay Swain

SKIING

For years I said it wasn't 'me'
My holidays were sun and sea
I knew I wouldn't take to it
Being the nervous type and not too fit
But John had to have the last word
And my objections just weren't heard
So extremely reluctantly
I booked a week in Italy
And now we're here and it's worse than ever
Will I come skiing again, *never, never*
My muscles ache from head to toe
And most of all I hate the snow
I can't stand up when in my skis
And if anyone else says 'Bend ze knees'
The weather is freezing, the wind cuts through
In just two seconds my hands go blue
I'm so unhappy I can't sleep at night
For God's sake someone get me on the next flight.

Jacqui Wratten

HOLIDAYS

The children are going on holiday
They are going to have some fun
They will all go to the seaside
Taken by dear old Mum

They take their buckets and their spades
To make castles in the sand
Mum and Dad will lay there
Listening to the band

Other people are swimming
In the deep blue sea
Mum and Dad they fancy
A nice strong cup of tea

Mum said to the eldest boy
Please take care of things
Any signs of trouble
Pick up the phone and wait until it rings

The police will come and help you
No matter what the trouble may be
I hope my boy is looking after them
Though he is only three.

Bert Booley

HOLIDAY MEMORIES

We heard the waters' angry roar,
As the surf beat on the sand,
And saw the majestic eagles soar,
As we strolled hand in hand.

In wonder we saw the waterfall's gleam,
And felt the glory of which we were a part,
I recall the moon's pure beam,
And the constant beat of my heart.

We saw heather's purple shades,
And mist on the mountainside,
As the sun's glory began to fade,
Making the peaks appear to hide.

We listened on the mountain,
Hearing the silence of eternity,
And as we turned back again,
We could feel the peace and tranquillity.

Now that time is over,
And the days of rest are gone,
But we will always be together,
With other such times to come.

Gill Sanbrooke

SUMMER HOLIDAY

It was beautiful abroad,
Boiling hot too!
Tunisia was fantastic -
The sea and sky were blue.

The sand was gold and tingly,
It tickled between my toes!
I wore my shocking-pink bathers -
'Cos it was too hot for clothes.

Those two weeks were special,
I will never forget
My wonderful Tunisian holiday -
I flew home on a Jumbo Jet!

Kelly Morris (8)

MEMORIES
(Dedicated to our daughter Mandy)

The flower may have faded but the seed of love still grows
In a secret place deep in our hearts that nobody else knows
You may have gone in person but your spirit is still here
Giving us fond memories now and every year
Your smile is in the sunshine your tears in the rain
We watch you on video dear daughter time and time again
Your laughter is in the wind, your sadness in the cloud
You were a wonderful daughter of whom we were so proud
You always had a smile for people everywhere
Even though a life of pain was the cross you had to bear
So each time a flower opens we see your smiling face
Photographs and memories that cannot be replaced
We always hear your whispers in the rustling of the leaves
Saying we must keep smiling, telling us not to grieve
It's hard not to darling daughter - you were the apple of our eye
We only hope God's taken you to that special place in the sky
So we try to keep on going until in heaven we meet again
Telling ourselves sweet memories will take away the pain
So until that day when we will knock on heaven's door
We we hold you in our hearts now and for evermore.

J M Harwood

THE SEASHORE

Let's have a stroll along the beach
and see the treasures there.
The golden sands within our reach
the tides to watch with care.

The sea goes out and leaves rock pools
where creatures safely wait.
Dog whelks move, sunshine rules
come on and don't be late.

Mussels and limpets cling to rocks
until the high tide comes.
Sea-urchins multi-coloured flocks
delight and join their chums.

Octopus, crabs and jelly-fish
amongst the seaweed hide.
Sea anemone and starfish
all to glimpse at high tide.

Pretty shells of all shades and style
jump out before our eyes.
Rippling waters bring forth a smile
when we wave our goodbyes.

Margaret Jackson

SANTA MONICA

Santa Monica winter's day.
Sun is sizzling bright.
Surf rolls in.
Bathers swim.
Our skin is very white.

Yachts glide over glistening sea.
Planes glide into sky.
Sunday dreamers on warm sand,
as roller-blades rush by.

'Bay Watch' babes
bare nearly all,
as other bodies bulge.
Black or white or brown skin.
A multicultural sprawl.

Ferris wheel turns slowly round.
It creaks and groans with pride.
LA County Lifeguard Team,
in pick-up, take a ride.

My boy, who plays at water's edge,
on wet and shiny sand.
Bending as in silhouette.
What treasures can he find?
Driftwood floating like a ship.
Imagination wild.

Seagulls mirrored on the sand,
then gliding, thoughts sublime.
And yet another plane takes off
to start its skyward climb.

Karen Knight

REMINISCING

As I sit on the rocks for the last time
Reminiscing about days gone by
Seems only yesterday since we arrived
And nothing seemed to go right at first
A smaller tent we did pitch overnight
I got a sleepless night, cold and wet
Which is just typical my luck!
The heavens opened up
And the wind was like corrugated sheets floating in the sky
Blowing a gale, but it was nice to be
Surrounded by sparkling gems high above.
It all seemed much better as the week went along
Chilling out on the beach as it got hotter
Snorkelling in the darkened waters avoiding the jelly-fish
Or mucking about in the inflatable dinghy
Days out visiting Totnes and Plymouth Dome
Dartmouth and Kingsbridge as well
The car breaking down and sitting by the roadside
Waiting for help to arrive
The heavy sea mist in the morning
When you could hardly see a thing
We had a good but unpredictable time
And as I walk along the pebbly beach
I will miss it all
But what I will miss most of all
Is being so close to the seashore
All I can do is reminisce
These memories of days shared together

Vanessa Salt

FINEST FASTEST FORTNIGHT

Lying by the poolside or on the sandy beach,
Away from home and daily chores our worries far from reach,
Relaxed and calm, warm and happy, just like having a dream,
Rise to shine whenever you choose, no alarm clocks or washing machine,

Foreign faces and voices, money and foreign food,
Not at all what you used to, stay longer if you could,
No jacket or jumper, not even socks, gloves - oh what are they?
It's even still warm in the evenings when the sun has gone away,

Home time - a drag, a depression, a thought,
You remember your chores conveniently forgot,
But the best time's been had when your mind thinks to, when . . .

. . . You get home you'll be booking for next year again!

Gillian Larkin

LLANDUDNO 1968

It's an old photograph, faded,
From twenty-eight summers gone by.
Great Horn - Llandudno 1968.
That's me there with those tufts of hairs
Looking like a little devil - which I was.
Front tooth missing, dislodged it a few days before,
Playing on that fire-engine climbing frame just over there.
Behind a tram creaking, snaking its way up the Horn
With a cargo, more, of holiday fun seekers.
Above high in the sky the all-too-new transportation,
Cable cars trundling along swinging in the breeze.
Father resplendent in Sunday best
And more importantly with a fistful of 99's.
Mother sadly now in what she would call,
That hideous dress,
Reading the Woman's Weekly.

Ian W Lyon

CHESHIRE

While you sleep in this half light,
I remember. I saw you shimmer
silent among the winds;
perfectly curved,
no sides at all to cut myself.
I came to you, gently.

You reached inside my closest grave,
natural beyond hope
that you could save my ghost.
You pulled me to your sure
and silently spoke till I was lost
in your adventure.

While you sleep in this half light,
it is strange. I feel your eyes burning
wild in fields and every sky,
and wherever you burn
your smile returns at last,
truer than April, softer than petals,
whispering still of our famous past.

While you sleep in this half light,
I look along your provinces;
the birdsong of your breath
descends the rise of your breasts
to the valley of your belly,
where I bathe and cleanse myself.

While you sleep in this half light,
I think I see forever . . .

Michael Pitt

68

HOLIDAY ROMANCE

A golden Prize in other
Men's eyes, he cast aside;
Now, cold as stone,
She weeps alone;
Promises all broken,
Empty words, and whispers
That were spoken,
Echo in her head;
All is dead;
Still she sees the sunlit
Happy days, the silver
Sands that time has
Washed away, and stealing
On the tide of Life, came
Sorrow, to devastate today,
And blight tomorrow.

Dorothy Neil

MEMORIES . . . LAKE ATTERSEE, AUSTRIA

Sadly I watched the sun so pink
Fade from the sky, behind mountains slink
My Austrian holiday was now nearly over
The coach would meet the ferry and we would see Dover.
Memories of views looking down from cable cars
Climbing high over trees, up, up, near the stars.
Thrilling moments had passed happily away
The end was nearing for this Saturday.

Daylight was fading, sky no longer blue,
Slowly slipping into a greyish hue
Twinkling lights of hotels, I could spy,
Gave a welcoming brightness to the darkening sky.

The little church on the hill gleaming so white
Tinged with gold from the surrounding floodlight.
Neat cosy wooden houses bedecked with red flowers
So breathtaking, in wonderment, I could gaze for hours.

The lawns so green, leading down to the lake,
With colourful blooms, no longer awake.
Rippling waters rolled towards me on the shore
This beautiful memory, so tranquil, I will store.

Alone I stood as I bid my sad farewell
Would I ever return, I wondered, who can tell?

Stella Bush-Payne

THE LAND OF PHARAOHS

Sunset over the mighty Nile.
I stood there gazing for a while.
The cruisers anchored for the night.
Their decks light up with floodlights bright.
And even now when I close my eyes.
That view from the balcony I visualise.

At Aswan there the mighty dam.
A contrasting work of modern man.
To the Cairo pyramids pointing to the sky.
The ancient Sphinx their heads held high.
The temples, massive, awesome, grand.
Dominating this enigmatic land.

And Cairo divided, new and old.
A wonderful city to behold.
The museum housing fabulous treasure.
The beauty of Tutankhamon's beyond all measure.
And even now I meditate.
And bring to mind those wonders great.

But despite the wealth in that fair land.
There's something hard to understand.
The peasants haven't changed their ways.
Still live as they did in Bible days.
Squatting in mud on the banks of the canals.
Sharing their huts with animals smells.

Now with winter drawing near.
I can look back on my memories dear.
And think how lucky I have been.
To see the things that I have seen.
They'll remain with me for ever more.
To reincarnate when life becomes a bore.

Ann Hargreaves

HOLIDAY IN RHODES

We went to see the Isle of Rhodes
And travelled many miles
We reached our destination
Our faces wreathed in smiles
The sun shone bright above us
The sea was shimmering blue
Everyone was happy
So many things to do
We planned to tour the island
To shop and see the sights
Byzantine churches, castles, harbours
And then - just overnight.
My back - oh dear, I couldn't walk
And nurse said - into bed.
And there was I - immobilised
Could only move my head.
But everyone was very kind
These strangers we had met
With good advice and lots of help
We never shall forget
Our holiday is over
We never saw the sights
Or visited the churches
Or walked the street of knights
A disappointing holiday
Not quite - for at the end
Those kindly strangers that we met
We now can call them - friends.

Lydia Barnett

AUSTRALIAN DREAM

Azure waves pound the sand,
Not a cloud scars the sky.
Pacific ocean reaches land,
See the dolphins surf close by.

Watch the parrots flying free,
In and out of vibrant trees.
How they do so love to be,
Sunning in such hot degrees.

Surfers carry boards, so keen,
No wet-suits needed in those depths.
Wet, bronzed skin, all a sheen,
They duck the waves, holding breaths.

Golden sands, stretch for miles,
Reaches South to Wollongong.
The nearest town so full of smiles,
Where hundreds work and battle on.

Schooners of beer, cold as ice,
Refresh the taste buds in the heat.
Everything here so very nice,
'Champions' the best bar on the street.

No need to cook, let's have a Bar-b,
Get those snags and beef steaks on.
That's all we lived on for our teas,
Plenty for all that came along.

We visited Sydney, saw the sights,
Flew to Queensland for three days.
Rarely had dull cloudy skies,
In Corrimal we liked to laze.

We stayed for a month and we did swear,
To return to Australia, a land so fair.

Mary Czornenkyj

NEVER AGAIN

All year we saved for our holiday time
Giving up sweets, beer and wine.
Economy meals had to eat,
No money over for any treats.
Told our friends, we're on a diet to slim
Even the dog and cat got thin.
It will be worth it in the long run
And can have so much fun.
The time came nearer and excitement grew
Bought second hand clothes, and nearly new.
Had done so well and saved almost enough,
Although the going was very tough,
Packed our cases for the trip
Thinking of sunshine and drink to sip.
Arrived in the rain, but it couldn't last
Soon in the heat we would bask.
It continued on though for two weeks
Like a river running through the streets.
So as we boarded back on the plane
Vowed, holidays to go on, Never Again!

Brenda Elvery

THE JOYS OF CAMPING

We opted for camping again this year,
So with great excitement we pack our gear,
We'd better pack a little more
to be on the safe side then I'll be sure.
The trailer tent is packed so full
I hope the car will manage to pull!
We leave very early to avoid the rush
but everyone else has the same idea.
What a lovely start to the holiday!
We arrived at the site, we've been here before,
We have a look round for a suitable pitch,
they're sloping or hilly, we'll have to wait
till somebody leaves but today they're all late.
Why did we choose camping again this year?
Off we set for a day to sight-see,
He decides to take the first park he found.
We got out of the car and had a look round
Where are the shops and centre of town?
'You'll just have to walk,' he's telling us now
all we could do was stay quiet and frown.
a half an hour later we reached the town
now all we want is to have a sit down.
After two weeks we pack to go home,
As the awning comes down we noticed a patch
it was the dog next door when taken short,
we've now got to wash it and wait till it dries
what a lovely end to the holiday!
At last we're home, that comfortable chair
and the full size bed, it's good to be home
But we'll probably go camping again next year!

Renate Margaretha Jarvis

POSTCARD

Dear Deborah,
the weathers hot
the sea is cool and clear.
The room is nice
though at the price,
a trifle much I fear.
The food is fine.
The view divine.
Yet but one regret my dear.
Dear Deborah,
sweet Deborah.
How I wish that you were here.

                    Yours discreetly
                    Thomas Wheatley

J N Roberts

ARIZONA DESERT

'Hide little javelina, from the hunter's gun.
To bag your tubby family, for him would seem like fun.'
How we gave a silent cheer when, tummies to the ground,
she led her family away, till they were safe and sound.

The Arizona Desert gave us many sights like these,
pretty red cardinals in the joshua trees.
Rabbits were dodging the prickly pear,
The ground dogs were hiding, but came up for air.

To lie in the swimming pool with sun on our cheeks,
but still watch the mountains with snow on their peaks.
The sun always shone in a deep azure sky,
the temperature soaring to 80+ high.

Could those black mountains really be true,
backing the slopes where the suagaro grew.
The cheeky roadrunner, with his cocky stance,
would share in our picnic if we gave him a chance.

So as I wash the dishes on this dismal Autumn day,
my mind's in Arizona many miles away.
The cacti around us on the dusty desert tracks,
the February sunshine glaring on our backs.

The desert's tranquillity made a perfect host,
to someone who went visiting from a far and distant coast.
For Catalina mountains and Wilderness I yearn,
so call me Arizona, and maybe I will return.

Brenda Gates

HAVE YOU BEEN THERE TOO?

Our holidays are typical. We teeter on the brink.
We leave it late to book our fate and take the kitchen sink.
We pack the clothes we never need, then freeze - or tend to burn
And every year we do the same! *Why do we never learn?*

The bronzed Adonis, free from stress adorns the brochure's ads
Angelic children seen, not heard, with smiling Mums and Dads . . .
Elite hotels . . . Now! They're for us. That chic unlived in feel.
We beg the tourist firm to flaunt its lowest cut-price deal.

The bargain bought we never thought to take the heavy hint
Of reading what the 'Package' meant in microscopic print.
Still locked in sleep, we soldier on as night rolls into day
And, true to form, we did not once *attempt* to lose our way.

Day one: We took some photos of the planes that made us quake
And managed to avoid the canny tradesman on the make.
No baking on the balcony. It's only just been planned
A twelve-foot drop awaits in ground that mimics golden sand.

Day two or is it *three* or *four*? The weather's turned so cool.
We've begged on bended knee for staff to sanitate the pool.
A most unseemly crack has cast a shadow on my wall.
It's really time to wonder why we've come out here at all.

Day five 'I'm going home.' This 'Leisure break' is best forgotten.
Then botulism struck a blow when food was served up rotten.
Some uninvited jelly fish recalled that we'd been stung.
The wall caved in. Our parting gift was, fittingly, a bung . . .
We bid farewell, with dented pride and blisters by the score.
We long for home and cups of tea, that welcome at the door.
We vow that compensation . . . that we'll never go again . . .
Until the skies erupt and spirits flag with all that rain.

Sylvia Williams

WATER UNDER THE BRIDGE

The inlaid stone said for all to see
That the bridge was built in 1612AD;
There over the wide and fast flowing river,
Even in that dry and hot summer.

I looked over the side and downstream,
To see the avenue of water move and gleam;
But I also heard a soft cascading sound.
From around the stone pillars barriers to the outward bound.

A natural music of a rippling melody;
Continuous and augmented with the echo
Of similar notes in timeless harmony
From the same score all those centuries ago.

A sudden gust of wind blew for a short time,
As often happens in a mountain valley;
And I was too late to parry
My brimmed straw hat blowing away from me.

Nothing could be done to retrieve the loss,
After an inward struggle I managed a silent laugh
For had I not wanted the civilised remoteness;
So nothing remiss to see the straw hat floating down the Dee.

Holidays must always come to their lamented end,
Work, duty, and urbanised friends renew their plea;
The homeward bend in the road leaves deep a nostalgic memory,
And the thought of a straw hat drifting out to sea.

Eric Ashwell

LAST RITES

Can I bear to see the ending of this day?
To be torn, silently screaming, from chequered fields and skewbald ponies,
from the protest of gulls and the grey-white tumble of cliffs and cottages
to the swishing taffeta sea.

Still in my ears, the burr-soft country greetings
'Well me beauty, 'tis another fine 'andsome morning.'
The squat green tugboat eases round the curve of the harbour,
angling the wharf-stones.

Will the gull with broken wing ever skim
again over the whipped cream wave-crests, on the rising current of the bay?
Now I will never know.

Along the creaming edge of today's docile wave
skips a child, firmly rounded as a hazel nut,
clutching a slanting kite on a bowed string.
A gull swoops curiously.

Eyes strain at the waning of the Cornish sun,
at the final glimpse of the last tossed wave, the last pouting sail.
Will my already shrinking soul ever fill again with the soft breeze from
the Point?

The joyous orange kite twists in final agony
and falls against the sun.

Dory Phillips

A SUMMER BREEZE

Whispering round my body
Light as butterfly wings
I revel in the silence -
Then a song thrush sings.

I can breathe the silence;
I can *taste* the sun . . .
Days that I've been dreaming of
Really *have* begun . . .

All the flower tubs blooming;
 - I've found time to laze
Summer lies before me
Stretched out in a haze.

Hannah Yates

HOW CAN I FORGET?

Inspired by something on TV
I said I have always longed to be
In climate cold and mountains bold,
Canada, that's the place for me.
So we took a 'plane
To Toronto, where we did the sights
For one day, then, at midnight
Made our way to train,
And took possession of a cosy coach
Where no other folk could encroach.
By day it was a living-room
With picture-window deep,
Then the steward settled us for sleep.
For food he did disturb,
To dining-car three times a day,
The scenery was superb.
As the train slowly chugged its way over snow
Through the Rockies we were to go.
Impressive grandeur, beauty, all of these,
Who knows how to describe
The magic of that stately drive.
We reached Vancouver, then off to airport
To fly to USA.
Where we were to stay for a while,
Then returned in style
To Vancouver and to roam,
Until we reluctantly found ourselves
On a 'plane for home.

F G Tester-Ellis

SPARE CHANGE OF SCENE

It's our holiday in London.
We do it every year.
A few days of gift buying
amid the Christmas cheer.

A holiday in London
with Christmas lights aglow,
tripping over youngsters
without a home to go.

It's Christmas time in London,
Harrods' shoppers looking neat,
spending cash, in contrast
to the beggars on the street.

A holiday of buying,
well, anything they'll sell.
Spare change into cold hands,
then back to our hotel.

Sights and shops, it's great.
How I hate to go away,
but rather that than staying,
sleeping in some cold doorway.

L C Evans

A NEW EXPERIENCE

A late holiday, it's just the tonic
to set us up for the winter ahead
A walking tour a new experience no
fancy clothes, just enough for a
rucksack, which can be carried
securely on your back!

Advice what should be taken, was
running at fever pitch.
A pair of good leather boots, with
several pairs of woollen socks
and a Kagoul was also needed
to complete the props.

A group of people from all walks
of life, to spend two weeks on
a walking tour, this seems to me
a very unrealistic thing to do.

A break for lunch, no restaurant out
here! Jam sandwich wash down
with clear fresh water from the stream,
let's pretend it's sparkling white wine,
well away out here, a person can dream.

Each night after a trek of fourteen miles
or so, we would reach our next destination
exhausted, with every bone in our body aching,
also blisters like golf balls appearing around
our toes.

Our guide has informed us, by next week
you will have become accustom to the hike.
This is a experience, I won't be repeating
not next year, or ever!

Esther Rehill

HASTE YE BACK

We used to go to sunny climes, where we had some happy times.
To Scotland we had never been, all that grandeur never seen.
To Edinburgh we made our way, to see the castle holding sway.
We took a stroll down Princes street and then of course saw Arthur's seat.
Across the Forth and into Fife, Dunfermline town and Bruce's strife.
Pitlochry, Callender and Perth, make a journey so well worth.
Pitlochry where the salmon leap, at whisky-making took a peep.
Balmoral next to see the Queen, hard luck! she had already been!
Crathie church, where Royals pray, shame it was a rainy day.
To Braemar where the games are seen, and once again, there was no Queen!
Aviemore where people ski, OK for them but not for me.
Culloden Field we tried to see, but too much rain, 'twas not to be!
Inverness and John O'Groats, how glad we were we'd got our coats.
No monster saw we in Loch Ness, and is there one? the answers 'yes.'
Ben Nevis is so very high, it seems to tower right in the sky.
Fort William next and then Glen Coe, MacDonalds met a nasty foe.
Ben Lomond stands beside the lake, which only time made us forsake.
To Stirling castle, Bannockburn, (Scots beat the English - so we learn!)
We saw the cave where Robert Bruce, once watched a spider on the loose.
To Gretna Green we made our way, saw where the Smithies had their day.
We're glad to Scotland we have been, the castles, mountains we have seen.
P'raps we'll go again next year but hope the weather's fine and clear.

Brenda Dawson

85

WHITESANDS BAY

A few faded photographs
Are all that remain,
Of a very special place
I'd love to see again.
Empty sands to play on,
So white, so smooth, so fine.
Calm blue water's stretching
To the far horizon line.
At night upon Rams Head
A crowd of us would sit,
We'd watch a darkening sky
That with a thousand stars was lit.
We'd sing our favourite songs,
Some new and some so old,
And many special dreams
And secret hopes were told.
We visited Saint David's,
A city that's so small,
With a beautiful cathedral
That has a steeple, oh so tall.
We went fishing in a boat,
Upon a sun kissed bay.
We played and laughed together
And had so much fun each day.
In Pembrokeshire, I'd love to go
To Whitesands Bay once more,
Revisiting those happy days;
Would make my spirits soar.

J Stephens

REMEMBER:-

Sunshine glistening on the sand
We strolled along there hand in hand;
Walking by the sparkling ocean,
Hypnotised by its gentle motion,
Warmed together by the sun,
Gently talking one to one.
Seeing beauty all around,
Joy in the comfort we had found.
Noticing no-one around about,
Blotting worldly cares right out.
No one there but you and me,
Such simple pleasures set us free.
June and sunlight, summer time,
Lulled by friendship's peaceful rhyme.
Trust is sewn and gently grows
From such memories as time bestows.
It flows within my heart and mind
Soothing all the hurt I find.
That summer day beside the sea
Will always mean so much to me.

Wendy P Frost

THE MAGIC OF MENORCA

A tiny little Emerald-stone.
Set in a sapphire sea,
The Island of Menorca
Lies in sweet serenity.
It holds a store of history;
Of Ancient conflicts past
And celebrates its Fiesta's
With excellent repast!
 But the magic of Menorca;
  I'm sure you will concur,
 Is the Ballet of the Butterflies
 In enchanted Pas-de-Deaux;
  And the rocking rolling tortoises
  Who crawl across the land;
  To dance 'neath waving palm-trees
  To a booming Cricket band!
  They all gather in the gardens;
  Of a Villa named St Pau,
  Just an easy journey -
 From the Capitol of Mao -
We count it quite a privilege
To make acquaintance too
And memories of our happy stay
Will help the Winter through.

Patricia Woodley

MEMORIES IN A BOTTLE

I unscrew the top of the suntan cream
And smell the lemon scent.
Inside this bottle half empty,
Holds secret memories spent.
I'm drifting now to far away
To a wonderful distant holiday.
The smell of orange groves fill the air,
Alfresco dinner for two to share.
Brown feet walking on foreign land,
Turquoise sea kissing sun drenched sand.
The peacefulness of the cool blue pool,
Reflecting the sun as a golden jewel.
Sunbather's tanning all shades of brown.
Sipping wine as the sun goes down.

Now standing here with this half empty cream,
I wake myself up
From this long distant dream.
Do I feel sad? morose? shed a tear?
Not me . . .
I'm planing a return of the
Same for next year!

Vanessa A Hulme

UPON LEAVING SKYE

Isle of my sorrows, Isle of my dreams,
To leave your shores is to die a little.
You are my nourishment and my healing.
Shrouded in your landscape of mystery,
Lost in your majestic peaks.
I am renewed, I am born once again.

To gaze upon your emerald skin,
To wash in your crystal waters,
To hear the flight of far off wings,
Is to enter a paradise of pureness,
At one with the order of nature.
The allure of a natural progression.

But leaving is my sadness,
It falls heavy upon my breast.
Your peace is but a cherished dream,
Your serenity a chaotic past.
I have tasted the grail waters,
I have passed through the mists of the Isle.

Michael A Williams

A POET'S PLACE

Among the lakes, their bright expanse,
How simple to dismiss, ignore
The traumas that had gone before,
Regrets that at my heart strings tore,
The rude results of risk, of chance.

The sloping breast of northern height
Encompassed me and let me dwell
With calm and I remember well
The Lake land's deep, hypnotic spell,
Its dawn of hope that banished night.

Wordsworth, precious, brilliant prince
Of poetry, endearing rhyme,
What finer ambience sublime
Might God provide, his power evince?
Sojourning there with blues and green
Painting a past and present too,
A feeling for creation grew
Whilst sharing bard's breath-taking view,
And empathetic thought had been

With versifiers, lake-inspired;
Such secret souls still lived for me;
Time had not passed and history
No supposition - I could see
And feel a magic wonder-fired.

Like other things it seemed must cease,
That quiet, Godly interlude,
The aura some suave ghosts imbued
Banished evils that intrude
Year long, the opposites to peace.

Ruth Daviat

AFTER THE FIESTA

What, little by little receding,
Clutched at your heart
Was not agricultural footstep
Going on home
To the tune of some troubadour plaint,
Was not the departure from Rome -
The terrible tread of the legions
Under the stars
Fading,
Was not even youth -
Its clamour repentantly loosed
Into an echoing forum
Whitened by age.

What, little by little, receding,
Clutched at your heart
Was the sombre tone of your lover
Reluctant to part,
So you sang of the peasants and fires
Anything frugal and sad
Suitably wide of the mark.

What, little by little, receding
Clutched at your heart
Was your own reluctance to know
What, little by little, receding
Clutched at your heart.

Alasdair Aston

NOT ABROAD

Playing with the children
fishing on the lake
going on a picnic
with sandwiches and cake
we didn't go on holiday
but we had fun all the same
we even had a day out
on a boat and then a train.
A holiday doesn't mean abroad
just togetherness and fun
so as far as I'm concerned
we had a brilliant one.

Dorothy Johnstone

I WALK ALL DAY

I walk along the beach
but the pebbles hurt my feet.
I have waited all year
for this seasonal treat.

I walk along the cliff top
and a wonderful view I see.
The wind is rough today
as it blows in from the sea.

I walk along the road
to go to the shops to buy my tea.
I will work up a good appetite.
I wonder what they will buy for me.

I walk back to our caravan
and as I've been very good
I will get a pat and a nice treat,
then I can go to sleep after my food.

I walk all day and at night
they put me to sleep in my little bed,
but then I creep in with them
to share their warmth for my weary head.

I walk in the sun and rain
just to keep them company.
I will please with a lick and cuddle
just because I am their gorgeous little Yorkie.

Rosemary Medland

ONCE UPON A HOLIDAY ... 1952

It was just another holiday
So thought my sister and me,
We'd spend a week at Butlin's camp
At Clacton by the sea.

Within an hour of reaching there
We two became a four,
Not what we expected
But most pleasant, I assure.

We kept each other company
Each day throughout our stay,
Enjoyed the days of sunshine
And danced the night away.

We left, with promises to write
When the holiday was done,
The postman was kept busy
With letters from each one.

The boys moved down to where we lived
From their homes quite far away,
The rapport that we had with them
Improved with every day.

A holiday romance can be fun
But will not last, they say,
Not long ago we proved them wrong
With Ruby Wedding Days.

Edna Cosby

EXODUS OF THE CABBAGE BUTTERFLY

*I*magine: vast bush-land, red soil,
Flatlands that pour before turmoil:
Of undulation, of ant-hill,
Of vistas serene, savage kill
Of things unseen; lurking there, death
And mirroring forms of life's fine breath.
*T*hen see: speckled white dots shimmering
 - African magic happening -
In a sudden birth - in millions -,
Butterflies, in God's dominions,
Wafting exodus-haze at play,
Endless mirage of just one day.

*P*alpable, urgent, death and strife
There on the wing for love of life.

Lloyd Carley-West

SUMMER HOLIDAYS

Some folk prefer to buy
A ticket for a plane
Then they wait for hours at Airports
For a crowded flight to Spain

Some would rather Hover
Or Chunnel through to France
Where they pay to use the beaches
Or see Can-Can Ladies dance

They go to Greece or Italy
Searching for the Sun
Where often it's too hot to move
To me, that's not much fun

Others choose Swiss Mountains
Or Swiss Lakes so blue and clear
Me? I prefer Mid-Wales
For we have it all, right here.

Bell Ferris

PHOTO FUN

I received my holiday snaps today,
Oh dear did I really dress that way,
With gaudy T-shirt and 'Kiss Me Quick' hat,
I can't believe I looked like that.

Here's one of gran strolling on the prom,
Pulling silly faces with great aplomb,
At home she's such a wise old sage,
But on holiday she never acts her age.

One of dad with a knotted hanky on his head,
To keep the sun from turning his bald pate red,
Mother in her bikini thinks she looks quite fair,
Who cares about the bulges here and there.

What's that sis won on the bingo,
Paid out far more than it's worth by jingo,
Why worry, have fun, and just be glad,
Holiday's the time to be a little mad.

Now we're back home and sensible as can be,
It's good to see the photos to stir our memory,
Of happy days spent by the sea in sun and rain,
Just think next year we can do it all again.

Pauline Wilkins

MOROCCO BOUND

To the kingdom of Morocco
Holiday makers flock,
A culture so different from our way of life
No fish and chips or rock.
The rugged vista of the atlas mountains
Beaches of fine golden sand,
Bazaars and markets alive with traders
Wanting to shake your hand.
Tapestries, leather, copper and brass
Carpets, almonds, mint tea,
You haggle a little to get a bargain
Only the scenery is free.
Museums housing fossilised skeletons
From prehistoric times,
Castles, mosques and palaces
Orange trees, lemons and limes.
Partridge, quail and wild boar
Are among the things to eat,
But sheeps' eyes are the delicacy
With which the Bedouin tribesmen greet.
Casablanca, Marrakesh, Tangiers and Rabat
All splendid in different ways,
A visit to Morocco
You will remember all your days.

Patricia Frampton

A MOMENT ON A SUMMER'S DAY

On a white hot day which made the sky
An azure blue and the trees greener, a butterfly
Dropped lazily onto the lawn to flit
Here and there tasting the sweetness of its favourite
Flowers; and, on spying the richer prize it sought,
Swooped swiftly upwards and was firmly caught
In the delicate silver of a spider's mesh.
Back and forth it beat its wings to thresh
In a frenzy seeking to regain the peace
Of the summer's day. But no release
From the web of death. Slowly, yet more slowly,
It fluttered until it became only
An inanimate, suspended wisp of desecration
Amidst the sunlight's exultation.

Rose Worms

COMING HOME

In England the wild hedgerows
are green again,
the drifting clouds
poor down on new mown hay
I have been so long away,
the farmland track
where I spent so many happy hours
is thick with blossom
after a shower of rain.

I no longer feel the pain of parting
because this time
I'm here to stay
and if I can have my way
will taste the English summer
once again,
my cottage windows
glint with evening sun
I'm feeling content when day is done.

Joan Hands

MASAI MARA

Dust and scrub,
Life in earnest,
Life in death.

Hyena travel,
Impala scutter-off into the distance -
Their irate tails whirring back and forth.

The lions laze in tangles of weariness -
They purr contentment.
Well-fed cats by the hearth,
Until . . .
A noise startle,
One moves, stalks his prey.
And the safari bus moves on - quickly!

Wendy Elson

MY HOLIDAY SPENT WITH MICHAEL

Holidays come and holidays go
But the last two were the best
I spent them with the man I love
When he asked me to be his guest

The first one was very exciting
Being together the whole of the time
Getting to know each other again
In a country where the weather is fine

The next year was even better
Going to another Greek island in May
This holiday was somewhat quieter
Spent relaxing for most of the day

Looking forward to the next vacation
It's called our winter break
Flying again from Stanstead
I'm so excited I just can't wait.

Susan Edwards

MEMORIES OF LOVE

She was standing with a map in hand
losing her way in the foreign land

the wind blowing her beautiful hair
she looked lovely and so fair

I could not resist approaching her
and made my services available to her

She shook her head from side to side
what to do next I had to quickly decide

I shrugged my shoulder and smiled
she put her finger on the map and also smiled

I understood she was from Germany
German words I knew but not many

Luckily I knew the town so well
I too was on holiday she could possibly tell

With sign language I told her to accompany me
to my surprise she agreed to come with me

Now that I became her guide
I walked with her by my side

I was as happy as Harry
this blonde I could marry

It was love at first sight
to win her I must get things right

Although language was such a barrier
being her guide made me merrier

At the time nothing mattered
but my dreams were quickly shattered

Approaching her was another man
and into his arms she quickly ran

Now back home I am dreaming of her
and am still in love with her.

Albert Moses

SEASIDE HEAVEN

The gentle sigh of breaking surf,
The heat haze o'er the sea,
The rolling shingles tinkling mirth,
All this is heav'n to me.

The shoreline sweeping round the bay,
The seagulls' plaintive call,
The happy children at their play
With quoits and coloured ball.

The waders on the sand-bank far,
The rock-pool's mystery,
The seaside rock; the shellfish bar,
All this is Heav'n to me.

Albert Hart

SWITZERLAND

The hills here were certainly alive but not with music but bells!
Large and small and made of brass they hug from necks of docile sandy
Cows as they munched on verdant grass.
In the distance an ornate church spire tolled for some to pray,
Goats nibbled, tails twitched urging pestering flies to go away.
Snow capped mountains enfolded the valley like huge protective hands,
Men in traditional dress their instruments gleaming played in the brass band.
Lots of talking, visitors in the 'wald' walking, farm cat in the meadow of
Sweet flowers a mouse is stalking.
Blue azure skies telling lies as grey clouds gather, breeze blowing, cattle
In anticipation are lowing,
Train on time of course toot toots, crack! From the woods as a hunter shoots!
Now it's the hunting season, they say with reason? I'll not eat the venison.
I'll nibble instead on warm crusty bread, drink crystal clear water from some
Ancient mountain spring hidden deep,
I'll breathe in pure mountain air, forget the mortgage, the bank manager
And the diet without remorse, I just don't care!
Wear no make-up, show my grey roots! Forget about my newly permed hair!
I'll wear tee shirts and unladylike 'trainers' chuck away my bra!
My Dior dress and perfume? They'll stay where they are!
Here in Switzerland this tiny land where the cattle really do roam
I'll soak it all up, fill my cup, until it's time to go home,
Then once again on my Yorkshire Moors I'll be at peace and sigh.

'There really is no place quite like home!'

J M Hefti-Whitney

THE HOLIDAY FROM HELL

A disaster from start to finish, the holiday made in Hell
We packed the car, we packed the kids, we packed the dog as well.
Then just as day was dawning, we quietly pulled off our drive
So as not to wake the neighbours, who still slumbered safe inside.

Halfway down the avenue, the kids were in full song,
But the car was growling tunelessly, clearly something wrong.
A judder, then a splutter, a dreadful terminal groan,
We all piled out, we turned around and pushed the beast back home.

The nice young man at the garage assured us we'd had a good deal.
Soon after lunch we set off again, with the aid of 'Rent a Wheel'.
We stopped for fuel, we stopped for the loo, and stopped for tea and toast.
The dog was sick, the kids fed up, it was dark when we reached the coast.

The landlady stood in the doorway of the 'Sea-view' B&B.
'You're late!' she told us sternly, 'You were due at half past three!'
Her hands rested on her ample hips, her warty face was set,
'I hope those kids are well behaved, and that's a well trained pet.'

Not the welcome we'd hoped for, after the day that we'd had,
Our room was damp, the beds were hard, the evening meal was bad.
We awoke bleary eyed next morning, threw open the window wide,
No sign of the sea, no sign of the sun, 'It's raining!' the children cried.

Not to be defeated, we trudged down to the sea and the sand,
With buckets and spades and flip-flops, fishing nets in hand.
A picnic box, an inflatable boat, a wind break and a kite,
Soaked to the skin we reached the beach, not another soul was in sight.

The dog ran round in circles like some demented pup.
Wet sand was flying everywhere, we put the brolly up.
The kids dug holes, collected shells and paddled in the sea,
And the donkeys stood with their backs to the wind as miserable as me.

Jane Lodge

SIDMOUTH INTERNATIONAL FOLK FESTIVAL

The flags are flying high on the ham,
Beneath them the steady beat of a bodhran.
In the marquee behind them is a tea dance;
Couples blending together by design or chance.
Down on the esplanade, bagpipes are heard;
Irish feet are darting so fast they are blurred.
White hankies of morris men flail in the air
And they crash their strong sticks as the devil they scare.
Garland dancers mirror the beauty of Spring,
While Bedlams enjoy the terror they bring.
Russian ladies glide with smooth elegance
Contrasting the Cossacks' explosion in dance.
A Welshman plays tangos crisply on his harp
And someone is singing with voice like a lark.
The market square rattles with cloggers so brisk,
Then rappers their swords and blithe bodies will twist.
The arena is crowded; the people all wait
In the amphitheatre in excited state,
Thinking of the sounds and the sights they'll enjoy:
Refreshing traditions that never will cloy.
Frenchmen dance on stilts while their brides thread beneath;
But Maoris dance flashing eyes, baring teeth.
An African wellie dance drums on the stage
Opposing apartheid, its message so sage.
Folk choir stirs emotion with tangible sound -
Escape into freedom from lives so work-bound.
A torch-light procession on the last night
Changes festival mood into darkness from light.
When holiday memories I wish to find,
These moments of happiness still swamp my mind.

Nicky Dicken-Fuller

PUERTO DE LA CRUZ

The jewel of the Canaries,
Whose climate seldom varies,
Is, oh so, magical,
To change would be tragical.

It lies on the northern side of the isle,
The ideal haven to rest awhile.
Hot days, warm evenings along the prom,
Different people, who knows where they're from?
A long cool drink in a pavement bar,
Relax among people from near and far.
Watch the warm, blue sea lash the land,
As it rolls over black rocks and black sand.

The locals who rush at a crawling pace,
Old ladies, veiled as they're making lace.
The flow of Spanish from a native of old,
Who hates to do what the Spanish have told.
The beauty of Tiede, the mountain so high,
Which dominates all under the sky.
Surrounded by sangria from prickly pear,
And as many bananas as one can bear.

To stroll around old, quaint shops,
And visit all the tourist stops.
The palm trees that grow everywhere,
Give welcome shade from solar glare.
The lava fields, so strange and eerie,
The sight of it, I could never weary.
I'll return again, that's my belief,
To the magic of Tenerife.

The jewel of the Canaries,
Whose climate seldom varies,
Is, oh so, magical,
To change would be tragical.

Philip Quinton Mills

AUGUST BLUE

The sky, the sea,
grey stones baked blue
by the oven heat.
A Greek enamel,
full of bleached sails,
besides which,
in dreams,
dolphins leap,
at arms reach.
August blue,
land, sea, air,
harmonise.

H R Burns

ROMANCE ON A PARIS COACH TRIP

During a stop for lunch,
I follow a hunch.
Casually prodding some brie with the end of my knife,
I ask
'Fancy a walk by the river?'
and cut off a sliver.
Then I butter bread madly
and inwardly groan at putting the question so badly.
But she replies, nodding
'That'll be nice.'
I bite on a slice.

M P Brown

THOSE HOLIDAY MEMORIES

Two weeks away, two years ago,
On holiday - off to France.
The sailing over
To Calais from Dover.
Aboard ship, drinking wine
And going off to dine.
Arriving at France,
An hour in advance.
And to the hotel
(The bed and breakfast from hell!)
Shopping,
'til dropping
And dancing - 'til morning!
sleeping at dawning.
Waking at noon
One week's gone so soon.
The clean golden beach
Beautiful forever
Dawning and setting
The sun, not forgetting -
The warm blue sea
Inviting me
The splash and play
On the hot summer's day.
Two weeks that flew so fast
Are now left in the past
But memories still remain -
Oh, to go back again!

Ffion Williams

CAMPIONI

Flocked shadows
sun etched me
in black

flutes sunlight
slanted through
the trees

in silence
I heard
birds wing beat

green curtains
drew back
silence touched me
here was a well.
Motes drifted
unknown moss

cushioned my feet
as I walked forward
water below

caught my eyes
reflected back, echoed.
I leant on stone

reality was lost
I became water -
drowned.

Teresa Webster

A DISTANT MEMORY

All ready to go the caravan hitched to the car.
Time we were off haven't got to go far.
We are just going down to the coast.
The outdoor life is what I like most.

I see so much scenery as I look about.
It's lovely just to hitch up and get out.
We are here now at Beacon Hill Park.
We better get sorted out before dark.

Just lazing around going at your own pace.
You always see a smiling friendly face.
Feet up let's have a cup of tea.
Then we'll go for a walk by the sea.

We meet this nice woman and man.
They tell us their names are Mary and Stan.
Scruffy is their dog's name.
He's okay he's quite tame.

We watched the yachts go sailing by.
It's so beautiful the birds singing and flying so high.
We visited the next towns and went for a long walk.
Just rambling along able to have a nice talk.

We came across a car boot sale.
Always bargains there let's look on this rail.
These kind of things I love looking around.
Ah! I'll have this it's a picture I have found.

At least we can look at the photos and remember.
Of wining and dining by the fire of burning ember.
And of course be looking forward to the next one.
Making sure it will be even much more fun.

Kathy Buckley

ON REFLECTION

I look out of my window and what is it I see?
A great expanse of water, blue - with waves so free
Sunshine filtering onto sand, children digging holes
Pebbles - seaweed - all abound, windbreaks held by poles
Ice-cream seller doing well . . . novelties galore
Sand and sunshine, fresh sea air, who could ask for more? . . .
I look out of my window and what is it I see?
A great expanse of concrete, a prison here for me
Rain comes down in torrents, children throwing stones
Rubbish all around us, sticks and stones break bones
The drug pusher is doing well, selling - killing too
Drinks and acrid smells of glue, someday they'll come to rue . . .
I look out of my window but I have closed the blind
Memories are hard to kiss when reality comes to mind . . .

Margarette L Damsell

THE HOLIDAY

When I was a child the sea was the
bluest in the world, sand in my shoes
the roll of waves covering my feet
the days of summer that brought such
joy.
Free from school and books the holiday
that fills my heart was Devon thatch
and winding lanes, endless days and shells
and stones, their colours still fill my
mind.
The secret places childhood finds, the
sparkling water running through my hands
picnics and lazy afternoons, the dreams that
children dream kept company with me till
morning, remembering that lost Summer I'm
that child again.

Catherine Neale

A SHOUT IN THE DARK

Southampton April 10th, at high noon tide.
It's 1912, it's unsinkable, it's unthinkable.
175 feet high, with four huge funnels.
First, second, third class, a ship built to last.
Super luxury and gracious attention.
Many hopes, far too few life boats.
Passing sighs, crowds wave their goodbyes.

Pleasure, relaxation, a maiden Atlantic voyage.
She steamed on, into the quiet starlit night.
14th April 11.40pm, her testimony the bitterly cold calm sea.
Iceberg warning calls.
Below the water, a curious motion,
On the starboard deck passengers collect, berg souvenirs.
The ship halted.

15th April 12.45am, the wireless, the first call.
'We are the Titanic sinking,
Please have your life boats ready.'
Constant rocket waves into a clear night sky,
Only the Carpathia steamed to save. 705.
The fabulous Atlantic liner began to slide
A pulling ocean her guide.

Women and children lowered in boats.
Behind, an ear splitting roar of steam
The ship quaked, the funnels churned.
2.18am the lights no longer burned.
2.20am 1500 souls, the playing band;
The gallant Captain Smiths last stand.
Unpredictability is never far from sure.

Anthony Keyes

THE GAMBIA

Corruption is as blatant as the sun
But the people have not been corrupted.
In their minds they practice honesty and peace . . .
A useful belief.

Julie Beech

WHERE DID WE GO THAT YEAR?

I can't remember where we went
But it was beside the sea.
The boys were only very small
And now they're six foot three!
I close my eyes and I can see
the gently lapping sea.
The palm trees waving overhead
Oh what a sight to see!
The boys are making sand pies
As happy as can be
I call to them to not go far
To be where I can see
The memories are so happy
But wait I think I know,
Was it when we went to 'Skeggy'
and stopped to see a show?

Valerie Roper

HOLIDAY TRAIN

I liked the train that travelled along
the Spanish coast.
That trip to Barcelona when the streets
began to roast.
The strange designs of Gaudi and Colombus
on his 'post'.
But I liked the train that took us, the most,
the most, the most.

Keith Roper

THINGS GO WRONG

Things go wrong every day,
In every house in every way.
When things go wrong it's a terrible sight,
When things go wrong people just fight.
Just picture this, you plan to go on holiday one fine day,
and it rains, it pours and it won't go away.
The car breaks down along a muddy track,
So you get out and push it nearly breaking your back.
Soon you are nearly there,
the children are crying and the wife's moaning about her hair.
You pray to the Lord to help you please,
you even get down on your knees.
Eventually you are nearly there,
people see you and they stare.
You think 'I know why they're staring at me, it's because
I'm muddy.'
Come to think of it, it is really funny.

Kerry Louise Hayley (15)

THE MALVERN HILLS

Where Elgar lies with freedom skies
Such beauty being all loves surprise
So close to heaven, so far from hell
You scream, you shout, but who would tell.

The rolling hills that dip and climb
What feet trod this soul of thine
What Secrets you could tell
Of lovers with such time to dwell.

As time goes by with such rush below
You seem to smile, you surely know
That when all is gone of mortal strife
This landscape of thine is truly life.

We rush about with so much to do
Money to make, business anew
No time for the present, future or past,
For some this day could be the last.

Stop for a moment, remember the time
You dearly loved someone with moments so fine
Look to the West across Worcester and see
The mirror of all life's destiny.

Walk to the peaks
Breathe air so divine
Make peace with yourself
Then return to your time.

D W Crump

THE BEE

A little girl on granny's knee,
Was fascinated by a bee.
She watched it fly into a tree.
Then lost to sight O deary me.

She waited, watched with baited breath
To see it reappear instead
It fluttered so very high
And disappeared into the sky.

E Kendall

CHEEKY THE MOUSE

There was an old lady who lived in a big house
One day she screamed when she saw a white mouse,
She flew through the air and stood on a chair
And said, what can I do? to get rid of you.

The mouse was cheeky he ran up, and down
So she put on her bonnet and hurried into town,
She bought a beautiful cat, he was black and white
He was named Scampie because he scampered all night.

You are no good she said I'll get another cat instead
So the next one was Georgie a very pretty one
But in the morning Cheeky was still on the run,
He even ran up the stairs and jumped on the bed.

The next cats were Tabatha, Lucky and Tom
Then Pudding and Peppi a large ginger one
At last Cheeky will be caught she thought to herself
But the little white mouse was fast asleep on the shelf.

Instead of catching Cheeky they all sat by the fire
And purred with delight, for the mouse they began to admire
As cheeky entertained them every night
By running up the curtains and swinging on the light

This rhyme has a happy ending after all
For Cheeky was such a loveable little mouse
They all lived happily ever after
In the old lady's house.

Mollie Carter

125

MISCHIEVOUS CAT

There was a cat climbed up a tree,
For here was the birds that he did see.
He tried to put his claws into the nest,
Go away you great big pest,
Squawked the mother bird let us be,
Cats do not belong in trees

The cat climbed down and walked away,
He left the birds until another day.
He decided they would wait,
As his food was on his plate,
Never mind I'll find a mouse.
To tease and catch around this house,
Heard of me in hey diddle diddle,
I'm the cat without the fiddle.

Christine Joan Rouse

MOON TRAIN

The moon came to earth for a ride on a train,
She said that she might like to do it again,
She didn't think much of the railway food,
And we all agreed that it's not very good.

She said that there wasn't much room in the seat,
Well she is rather large with incredible feet,
And the people stared so as she sat in that train,
So we said, 'If it bothers you, you should complain.'

To be fair though, it is rather rare that you see
The moon on a train, bound for Hayle or Dundee,
A comet occasionally, maybe a star,
But when it's the moon, you don't know where you are.

So smile, be polite and use your good sense,
And don't do a thing that could cause her offence,
Or she'll leave in a huff and go back to the sky,
You think this is nonsense? My dear, so do I.

Nick Spargo

TEDDY BEAR LOST

Teddy bear, teddy bear where are you,
I put you down for a minute or two
To play with Barbie, and little sweet pea,
Then mummy called it was time for tea.
I looked in the cupboard, and under the chair,
Looked in the toy box, but you were not there,
Then under the bed, saw a twinkling eye,
So I sang to you a lullaby.

Janice Richer

THINKING OF YOU

Oppressive summer days make me inert;
Autumn's benign smile, smoothes her distress:

The time is dull, but may erupt
though I ever notice
she wears fresh beauty in sad years.

Mystery of her young days
trauma in her life unseen:
am I late too involved to know
or, am I just a fool,
not to invade her life too soon.

If I knew young plight
but then, am I the judge.
Try not to be insensitive.

Herbert Wilson

SCOTTISH HOLIDAY

Crags rise into the azure sky,
Sheep climb on the peaks on high,
The golden rays of the setting sun
When another day is done,
Turn their hues to purple and pink,
Above the loch where cattle drink,
And at their reflections stare
In the shining water there.
Mallard and swans drift idly by
And I hear their lonely cry.
Motor-boats skim noisily past
And silent darkness falls at last.

Ruth Margaret Rhodes

BANK HOLIDAY

Summer time, Bank Holiday,
Traffic everywhere,
With caravans and boats and tents,
All heading for sea air.

The weather's hot, red and white cones
Stretch, far as can be seen
We're stuck amid the miles on wheels
With just a flask of tea.

Stuck here in this stifled car
The children start to cry.
'Are we nearly there Dad?'
Mother heaves a sigh.

At last we reach our destination,
Tired, with tempers frayed.
We park the car beside the sea
To let the children play.

'Can I have an ice-cream Dad,
A bucket and a spade,
A sun hat and a pair of shorts?'
(Of money I'm not made!)

This is just the first day
And my wallet's looking sparse
And all I really want is just
A cool beer in a glass.

But just for now, I'll sit down
In a deck-chair by the sea
And close my eyes, perchance to dream
Of peace, tranquillity . . .

Mary Brooke

THE HOLIDAY THAT WAS A WASH OUT (1980)

When I arrived in Rome
A long way from home
It was pouring down with rain
I could not believe my eyes
So I took a look again.

The crew lined up to say goodbye
I looked the pilot in the eye.
Were you the driver? I enquired humorously
Is this sunny Italy?

'I was indeed the *driver*' he replied
'But, the weather's not down to me.'
It rained and rained both day and night
I got drenched and looked a sight!

Arriving in Capri my husband and I
Walked to the top
Slogging away, not knowing
A vinicular could have taken us all the way!

Next we received a telegram to say
My mother-in-law had died that day
Our holiday had been muddy, not dusty
I returned home, not tanned, but rusty!

Rita Hughes-Rowlands

A LOST DREAM!

Oh, what a beautiful scene!
So quiet and so serene.
I was walking through a meadow green,
So peaceful nobody had ever seen!

The only sound, a singing humming bird,
Nearby, a river rushing along, most weird!
Gambolling white fleecy lambs,
In the distance, footsteps on sands.

By the cops, across the stream,
A swaying shadow could be seen!
Walking slowly over the bridge,
Disappearing into the forest, by the ridge

Could have been a shepherd, tending his flock?
Resting in the shade, by the rock.
On the horizon, the evening sun,
Quietly bidding good-bye, to all the fun!

The luscious, long, green grass for hay,
Dotted with wild flowers, in May!
White daisies for a chain, near the pathway!
Even the bees were humming noisily away!

Suddenly the echoes of a dog's bark,
Awoke me from my dream, still in the dark!
How sad! To wake, not where you have been,
So wonderful, somewhere in your dreams!

To come back to this life, oh so real!
Yesterday has gone, all lost in a *Dream*!

Eva Rose

MEMORIES OF A HOLIDAY DISCO

I listen to the tape of songs to which we danced
Fourteen years ago in our holiday romance.
They take me back to the holiday camp disco
At Prestatyn by the sea so long ago.

You stood there in your pretty red dress
With your sister beside you and I was impressed
By the photograph you stole from me and which you did hide.

So I have not your picture but the tape I can hear
Of songs that were hits in that far distant year
I think of you, your age the same as mine,
You were fifteen then, now you'll be twenty nine.

Have you been educated? Did you get a degree?
Did you go to university?
Are you married with children? Are you single like me?
Whatever you're doing I hope you're happy.

Malcolm Lisle

AOTEAROA

Whisked one day
On a high speed jet
To a place far away
I'll never forget

Volcanic cones
And lava tunnels
Rangitoto Island
A joy to explore

Blue green lakes
Of steaming water
Bubbling and gurgling
Like pans on the boil.

Ketetahi hot springs
Silently steaming
Out of the rocks
And into the sky.

Glow worms all twinkling
Like tiny green stars
All in the caves
At Waitomo èn route.

Mountains and trees
So still and serene
Mirrored in lakes
A beautiful blue/green.

New Zealand for me
Adventures galore
I'll always remember
But I'd like to see more!

Kathleen Barker

PROVIDENTIAL ANGER?

The echoes of the raging seas
The fateful cry of gulls in the bay
Where e'er it listeth, the brave gale blows
Sweeping all *my* fears away.

The outrageous wonder, the splendour of it all!
Sheer loneliness of the mighty waves
The grandeur, and perpetual motion
Eternal beauty the way the sea behaves.

Was it like this in ancient times
When God beheld old Adam's fall?
The thunderous skies, in a sense the beauty
God's anger unleashed upon us all?

Mary Hayworth

DISTANT OASIS

footprints in the sand
a photographic reminder of desert bliss
lost amid the Pyramids
you led me by the hand and kissed
the woman inside
you said you loved me 'like a flower'
I opened to these wistful words
and our holiday secret was kept forever
in a picture of clasped hands

although the holiday was over too soon
memory waves its magic wand
as you walk like an Egyptian
across the desert of my mind
and I reach out delicate for that distant oasis
buried forever in the sands sublime
where an hourglass on my cabinet
brings back the whispered place and time.

Julie Ashpool

AUSTRIAN SOLITUDE

The fresh clean air floats down the mountainside
and fills the depths of the patchwork valleys.
Meadow-green grass waves in the breeze.
The sun beams down and is reflected
in the dazzling petal power cradled within.
The gaze is taken to the furthest, most distant heights.
Emerald forests,
cotton-wool islands, that cling perilously
to the startling slopes,
border the communities of solitude.
Peace pervades
and stillness can be found and almost touched.
The roads lead on,
zig-zagging pathways -
to a new and unreal world, high in the sky.
As I look upward and capture the moment,
I wonder if dreamers are watching from above.

Bettina Jones

AMBITION REALISED

There's a special smell to an Indian crowd,
Coconut oil and fruit.
Horns and music incredibly loud,
Overfilled drains pollute.
Fighting your way through hawkers' hands,
Goods at inflated price,
Regretfully evading the begging bands,
Pence for a bowl of rice.
Squeeze through an ancient battered door,
Into a sandstone aisle -
Down pressed heat filters red to the floor,
Turrets rise in Moghul style.
Through an arch with inserts, curly Koran quotes,
The shimmering vision appears,
Above symmetrical gardens a cloud floats,
The wondering crowd reveres.
Doubled image reflected in the lake,
Eye-dazzlingly white,
Greater love could no human make,
For centuries kept bright.
Fifty years since I left with the Raj,
Memories flood in from youth,
A long held ambition to see the 'Taj',
A world's wonder in truth.

Di Bagshawe

THE SUMMER HAS GONE

Tearing at my tears
in the chill of the wind
breaking down the years
as the summer ends
August dream-lost and gone

It all comes to an end
now that the summer has gone
It all comes to an end
with the last song
The Summer has Gone

But I will remember
those secret tears
Lost alone in the summer years
seven days before the Fall
seasons change
in the shadow of rain
Autumn leaves turn and bleed
in the colour of veins

A last kiss good-bye
as I turn to watch you go
A last glimpse
As your smile turns to gold
Distant memories as the summer fades
with a September flame

So many feelings
Broken and Cold
In a dying world
that fights my fold
It all comes to an end
Now that the summer has gone.

George Harrison

ROCHDALE OR ROUSSILLON?

Bleak, rain soaked, wintry Rochdale,
Smiling, sunny, summery Roussillon's antipodes,
Where hearts, sleet-frozen,
Yearn for warmth and shimmering azure seas,
Oppressed by Bright's slag-grey,
Lowering misery clouds.
A three day nightmare in a sweaty car,
Or broiler-chickened on the Motor Rail,
Could see me basking on the beach at Canet-Plage.
But I fly to the sun through Asda's doors,
In Tesco's, Morrison's aisles my tickets lie.
I quaff the Fitou, Caramany,
La Chênaie, Côtes du Roussillon village,
Mas Sibade,
And dream I lie at Argelès,
Yearning for strains of 'Sally', sounding brass,
Pine for Thompson's fish and chips,
A pint of Thwaites or moorland peace,
Amid the Gallic clatter of the Mickey Club.

Alan Swift

REFLECTIONS ON THE LAKES

Looking back on the Italian lakes
Sometimes seems like a dream
Of blue waters like satin on green velvet trees
All part of nature's scheme.

Of dramatic mountains
Climbing up to the sky
And pretty islands nestling
With boats sailing by.

Whose 'Old Town' streets
Are cobbled and coarse
Built for the age
Of the carriage and horse.

Cascades of flowers
Come tumbling down
Over wrought iron balconies
Of houses yellow and brown.

The lakes sparkle like diamonds
Reflecting the sun
Amidst beautiful gardens
Enjoyed by everyone.

I leave you with the picture
As I say goodbye
Of azure lakes and mountains
Silhouetted against the sky.

Barbara Fosh

PRICKLY PEARS AND PIAGGIOS

Prickly pears and Piaggios; friendly people too,
Bright sunshine, beaches white, skies of deepest blue.
Pink flamingos beside the roads, on glittering silver ponds
And everywhere the tall bamboos wave their graceful fronds.
Ancient Roman ruins at a wonderful place called Nora,
Hillsides teeming, colourfully, with exotic local flora.
At Palau and La Maddalena we lingered long to potter,
Then on to Costa Paradiso's rugged rocks of terracotta,
We saw the Emerald Coast, where the rich and those well known
Lounge in elegant splendour, stretching out their idle bones.
Busy local markets; walls sporting graffiti bright,
Elegant shops in Cagliari, marble floored, so cool and light.
A cheerful fruit vendelo daily sells his wares
Along avenues of cacti that are known as prickly pears.
A Giant's rocky tomb, far up on mountain high
In peace stands eternally against the changing sky.
Three wheeled Piaggios; and scooters laden with family of four
Expertly weaving a way through the busy traffic's roar.
Oh beautiful Sardinia, where it was so easy to unwind,
These memories, so vivid, live for ever in my mind.

Margaret Gower

NOSTALGIA

Back to memory
Comes a Cyprus holiday
Not so long ago

I had been before
All of fifty years ago
And I enjoyed it

This time, different
The hospitable people
Were ever the same

But a cloud was there
We were barred from visiting
Some places I knew

We could stand and look
Far across the barrier
Of rifle and steel

Nostalgia was there
Remembering long ago
What Cyprus was then

Half a holiday
Was very enjoyable
But I remember

John Carter-Dolman

THAT TRANQUIL PARADISE

'A tranquil paradise,' said the travel agent
'A beautiful setting, long sandy coves
A haven for *discerning* holiday makers,
Away from those touristy droves.'

The taxi left at twelve,
And we switched on our holiday torch,
To see thousands of buzzy mosquitoes
Partying on our porch.

The studio was so cramped and small
That it should have been called a 'stu'.
And when the cockroaches waved 'hello'
We didn't know what to do.

I slept sitting up in my clothes
Tired, with tear-stained cheeks.
Was this hovel the heavenly paradise
For which we'd been saving for weeks?

I could see nothing around for miles,
When the next day dawned anew,
Except scrubland and a dot on the horizon
Which may or may not have been blue.

We had 'a word' with the rep,
From the *discerning* tour operator;
Perhaps instead of a welcome pack
They should have left a detonator.

Insist on full information
And spare that holiday despair,
If a tranquil paradise is recommended,
Discerning holiday makers - beware.

Katriona Hart

BETHANY BAY ... USA

Creamy shore, where snowy waves
Breaking long, with rippling rolls
Serve the sandpiper with tasty food.

Tripping, twinkle-toed he steps
Daintily along the curling edge.
His sharpened beak stabs swiftly down
Making minute holes in floury sand
Whilst stately seagulls stroll the strand.

When thunderous breakers crash and roar
And mortal eyes grow strangely sore
Striving and staring o'er limitless span
Of sinister ocean, grey and green;

Still, along the curling water's edge
Toes daintily dabbling in the shallows and sand,
The solitary sandpiper swings sight back
To measurable, pleasurable witness
Of nature's form.

Deirdre White

VOLCANIC SELF

Like a volcano, you and I;
    A mountain
With inner core
    So deep, unfathomed,
To surface, then,
    From time to time.
Layers of rock
    And vegetation
Cramp my style.

Like a volcano, you and I;
    Raw and explosive
Red-hot, molten rocks
    Steam and sulph-furious ash
Spewing, spitting, hissing out.

Like a volcano, you and I;
    One minute
Gently warming the world
    Of space and time, and thought
With springs of mineral water
    Gushing or cascading out,
And the next?
    Changing whole landscapes, seascapes,
With red-hot molten lava,
    Flowing downwards, forwards, onwards, ever . . .

Like a volcano, you and I;
    Deep and unknown,
Even to ourselves;
    Savagely shocking, sometimes soothing
The world of thought and time and space;
    Volcano you . . . and I?

Joyce Bridle

DISTANT MEMORIES

Now it's winter I'm back in Suburia
where it's esoteric and cold
When it was summer you could walk
Bare chested, it brings out the
Insoucia once in one, you could be bold
Ah it didn't seem long when I was
Sunning myself on a lovely beach
Where beautiful girls in bikinis
Were never far out of reach
But there you were, we were in love
When our doe eyes met
Strolling hand in hand on a beach
Desolate.
Now it's back to reality when
Everything seems so dour, so serious
While on holiday we were allowed
To be frivolous.

Gary Gibbs

OVER AGAIN

'Twas only this year
Yet seems long ago.
I sat on my own
And was so full of woe.
My husband had left me
For another female
After 38 years of a life so real.
He's gone I said to my little dog
Whose love was so strong
I just had to live
So I sat up straight and rang my friend
How would you like a holiday I said.
It it's not too dear came the happy reply
I'll see you later she said to I.
We met we discussed we decided 'yes'
So on the 20th of May
We set off on our holiday.
'Twas Butlins we said
At a place called Minehead
And that was a turning point.
It was the time to change my life
But I didn't know at the time
He stood in the doorway of his chalet
He said good morning as we passed his way
And we met him again the very next day.
My friend must have noticed something I did not
If you like to be alone, I said eh what?
But she insisted, I'll go back the day before
We had to return. I said you won't
To the chalet she went and Norman walked me back
And now I'm engaged to this man who was there
At that chalet in Minehead. I'll love till I die.

Florence Brice

149

ONCE UPON A HOLIDAY

We went to the seaside,
For the fresh, salty, sea air,
To watch the incoming tide,
And relax, under the sun's warming glare.

Elegant sandcastles, rose from the sands,
As we flip-flopped about the beach,
Buckets and spades in diligent young hands,
The now ebbing tide, out of reach.

The melting liquid ice-cream,
Trickles down stale yellow cones,
As sticky fingers become part of the scheme,
Along with Victorian tea rooms, trading in scones.

The dream is now lost forever,
As ghetto blasters break the peace,
Where the tea rooms once boxed clever,
Arcades now abound, like a noisy disease.

Exhaust fumes for sea breezes,
Hot dogs or burgers, for cream cakes,
High pollen, hay feverish sneezes,
And mad cows, eating mad cow steaks.

Kiss-Me-Quick hats, instead of boaters,
Kamikaze wasps, dive-bomb passers-by,
The sea awash, with inflatable floaters,
Noisy tourists, screaming hi-de-hi!

At last, a pleasurable peace,
Like the ebbing tide's foam,
And finally, the ultimate release,
In the comfort, of our own home.

Jeremy Bloomfield

WHICH MEMORY

I see her still sitting on a drystone wall in the Cotswolds
Or walking her face held into the salt-wind upon a Cornish beach
Flowers coloured as by a magic wand
Waterfowl no less so upon a pond

The open vista of a Devon moor
And items purchased at a village store
Or perhaps trout lively in a roadside stream
Or was it the special meal with home-made ice-cream

Ah perhaps it was the Wurlitzer show
Or the setting sun with its fiery glow

The memories held no other can know
Nor holiday films or snaps show

Clive Cornwall

YORKSHIRE MOORS

The brown and green and autumn gold
of heather and ferns in the distance unfold.

Each bend in the road brings expectations
of moors and trails for explorations.

The car park is full of anoraks and boots
of walkers deciding on their various routes.

A quiet excitement pervades the group
their packs are bouncing when off they troop

A quiet and steady crunch, crunch, crunch
as they all leave together in an orderly bunch.

Through prickling bracken and dying ferns
far away in the distance, cry gulls and terns.

The sea is just visible, sparkling and grey
it all adds up to a satisfactory day.

A lunch time stop is eagerly taken
with sandwiches to eat of eggs and bacon.

An apple, banana or maybe a pear
a block of chocolate for those who dare.

A pint in a pub would be right for drinking
but out on the moors it is wishful thinking.

Quiet talking can often be heard
or maybe the cry of a hidden bird.

Colours are continually changing ahead
clouds rushing past, the sun growing red.

Evening is creeping over the hill
The wind blowing up with a biting chill.

Time to return for a hot bath and a meal
to chatter and laugh and say how we feel.

Unfortunately nothing forever will last
and memories gradually fade into the past.

Judith D Palser

DAYS AND HOLIDAYS

I remember long ago
of holidays I've taken
must be 50 years or so
in places long forsaken

It was such a hassle then
with kids and dogs and such
what with luggage, toys and dog food
we needed oh so much

But now there's just the two of us
we only need one case
it's all posh frocks and evening wear
we even go by bus

But standing on those open shores
I often hear ghost voices
and see the children's happy smiles
not empty sands for miles and miles

I see my long gone much loved dog
deliriously happy
chasing waves and digging sand
but now, all dogs are banned

If I could have back just one day
to live again the joy
the future then we could not see
now we're strangers them and me

We don't let them know how lonely
old age days can be
we sit wrapped up and see the ghosts
while gazing out to sea!

Greta Edwards

HOLIDAY

How I miss the sand,
How I miss the sea,
How I miss the sun,
We had on holiday.
The lazy morning walks,
Our lunch eaten in the park,
The long lazy afternoon,
Warm from our long talks,
Of days to come,
Of days gone by,
On this our holiday.
How I'm glad we came away,
How I'd love to stay,
And live along the coast,
This is what I want, the most,
But soon we'll get home,
You, the kids and me,
Home and the memories of our holiday,
With holiday snaps to show the family.

Diane Campbell

MOSI-OA-TUNYA
THE SMOKE THAT THUNDERS

The sun beams down on Victoria Falls
With its sheer rock faces forming its walls.
Mosi-oa-Tunya its African name
Though David Livingstone took all the fame.
He named it after the queen of our land
Looking east on the Falls his statue stands.
Hear the mighty roar as the spray clouds rain
See the boiling smoke that thunders untamed.
Touch the leaves' wetness in jungle surround
Smell the rich earth where its creatures abound.
Taste rainforest drops on lips ever moist
Speech is drowned out as its splendours are voiced.
Rainbows appear in surrealist mist
As perpetual spray, fountains and twists.
Winding Zambesi drops over the edge,
Bounces, explodes over many a ledge.
Long and mysterious canyon so deep
Where river tributaries flow then leap.
Water cascades like a curtain so long
To gullies below where the boulders throng.
The Rainbow Bridge arches over the gorge
As way below dare-devil rafters forge.
In pliable craft white water they fight
Into raging foam they vanish from sight.
Admire its beauty that changes each hour
Exquisite in sunrise or sunset's power.
Zimbabwe's gem on its border they share
With Zambian folk admiring it there.

Jan Claxton

ONE LOVELY WEEK IN AUGUST

There are some milestones in our memories
Where Dorset welcomed us into her arms,
So we could sense the profound melodies
In ancient cottages and peaceful farms,
Calm in spite of tourists who came to gaze
In awe at a world perceived in a dream
As a benign spirit beyond the haze
Revealed the glory in a crystal stream
Of pure water from the sweet font of life
That led us on to the august abbey
And Sherburne was like a devoted wife
Who polished our auras. They were so shabby!
Which informs us we must go there again
And forsake our sunny castles in Spain.

Patricia Howe

157

SWEET SOUNDS AND TECHNICOLOUR DREAMS

So you wanna be a country star
With a dream in your head and a cheap guitar
With a handful of songs and no place to play
You leave for the lights of the USA.

So you wanna be a country star
But to make the grade you gotta play the bars
On Music Row in this music town
Is where the spirit of *Country's* found.

So you wanna be a country star
With snakeskin boots and sixteen cars
But down on real street times are tough
'Cos strumming for tips never pays enough.

So you wanna be a country star
And blend in the crowd where the greatest are
Like Campbell and Cash and Parton and Young
The legends live on and the songs are still sung.

So you wanna be a country star
Drinking shots of Jack D down at Tootsie's bar
With misty-eyed visions of seeing your name
Engraved on a plaque in the grand Hall of Fame.

So you wanna be a country star
With a dream in your head and a cheap guitar
But a dream with a smile it will always be
To remind me of Nashville, Tennessee.

David Harrison

VACATION'S OVER

Vacations over goodbye to the sun
It's back to my business there's work to be done
Through rush hour traffic ears deafened by noise
I'm thinking about girls but am surrounded by boys

The sand on the beach is now a carpeted floor
My suntan's now fading to as pale as before
The girls in bikinis watched playing at ball
Are now only pictures on my locker wall

The drinks in the night club and their cabaret queen
Replaced by the tea girl in our works canteen
The rush of the surf so soft to the ears
Now the hum of computers now is all that I hear

My vacations over goodbye to the sun
I'm back at my business and this work is no fun
Yes vacations over goodbye to the sun
But I'll be back when another year's done

Don Woods

AN ODE TO HAPPY HOLIDAYS

I sit at home and remember the day,
When my family last went on holiday,
Gong away and leaving the rat race behind,
Sitting on a sunny beach a chance to unwind,
Enjoying the change and the sunny weather,
Feeling so glad that the family were together.
Then suddenly, I remember what it was really like,
When the cases fell off the roof rack and into the drive,
Sitting on the back seat, listening to granny moan,
Being sick out of the car window and hearing the driver groan,
Being driven there at high speed and gripping the seat,
Arriving suddenly and missing the ground below my feet,
Moving around me at what resembles a concentration camp, a horrid place,
With chalets packed closely together in a very confined space,
I compare it to the brochure photograph,
Which the place doesn't resemble at all,
I step through the front door and put my hand through the wall,
The chalet is dirty and the worst I have ever seen,
And I grab one of the dusters and attempt to clean,
The rain outside, starts to pour,
As it drips from the ceiling and trickles down the wall,
It is at last the next day and it's really sunny and hot,
And I start to scratch where an ant bit me, it was a good shot,
I sit down upon a very stony pebble beach and start to go very red,
And spend the next day with blisters and sun burn on my head.
It is half way through the week, and I've been
Marking off the days, until we can go home,
As all I ever hear outside is building noise, kids and people moan,
At last, that day is here and I leap into the car,
Which decides to have a break down and we don't get very far,
We are towed back to the holiday camp, to wait for the car to be repaired,
Counting what's left of our holiday money,
Because the bill will have to be shared,
We arrive home at last and I will never go on holiday again,
Not even if someone paid me a million, but maybe I will for ten.

Emma Kemm

CYPRUS

It's said all good things must end
If only I had the money to spend
A villa I'd buy on top of a hill
Where orange groves are growing still

Oh Cyprus, you sunny isle
With your beauty you, me beguile
Hills alive with olive trees
Your dark mountains, and bluest of seas

Your friendly people who smile and wave
As we pass by every day
Generosity to a fault
Your ways I wish I'd been taught

How I wish I was there still
To watch the sunset between the hills
See the lights glow in the valley below
All this beauty on you God did bestow

Pamela Smith

A CRUSADING MEMORY

There on a trip to Anotolia
we knew not that this place was Holier,
for here had Paul and John resided,
within the place we had bided.

Now Ephesus, that City of Ephesians
is mentioned in the New Testament, for guidance,
that here had John and Jesus' Mother
had set up residence, and to recover.

That here they stayed after the Resurrection,
that advice to John, from the crucified One.
'Take thee my mother too thy family,'
and now it is here that two Popes paid homily.

Within the town of Selcjuk, Anatolia,
you can see St John's Basilica,
and high in the hills, where the eyes traverse,
a stone built house, stands on the mountains obverse.

This little house, holding a Black Madonna,
crucifixes, prayers and all we honour.
It is there for all to see and visit,
a reminder of a time and unflinching spirit.

Alan Noble

THE ISLAND COTTAGE

From the still Loch Slapin waters
I see the bulk of Blaven rise,
And where the mountain peaks slope down
The island cottage lies.

In summer the daisied meadows
Dew-pearled in the opal dawn,
Through their waving grasses ripple
White and gold in the island sun.

This is a secret island
Stained with many a dark deed done,
Bedevilled by superstitious fears -
Stirred by tales of battles won.

In the island today there is healing
From each purple mountain and moor,
Along winding paths, by singing streams
And the marram-reeded shore.

It was the cottage of my dreams
I had never thought to see,
Flanked by flowering meadows
And facing the small isles of the sea.

Eileen King

ANCHORS AWAY

Was it just a month ago
We were lazing in the sun
Not a care in all the world
Our holiday had begun

Boating on the Norfolk Broads
Fishing all day long
What a life of luxury
As we happily sailed along

Enjoying all the wildlife
And the peace and quiet
Escaping from the city life
The pollution and the riot

The vacation went too quickly
It doesn't really seem
As if we ever went away
It's like a distant dream

Now, alas it's over
Back to work, I fear
Just to earn an honest crust
So we can go again next year

Lynn Williams

A SUMMER TIME

Summer is made of skies so blue,
and lazing around with much to do.
Sun kisses beds of flowers so bright,
and imperfection out of sight.

Wining and dining and night time charades,
these perfect days that come custom-made.
Young buds of summer swell in the sun,
long days on the beach with lots of fun.

Browning legs and tanning arms,
the smells of fruit and suntan balms.
Long lasting days of summer heat,
these are the days impossible to beat.

So when I leave this Earth so true,
let it not be on a day of blue.
But on a day where the sun shines high,
so my soul will rise into a sunkissed sky.

Emma Wells

(INNELLEN) OUR HOLIDAY

We set out on our holiday
The car packed - the house all checked
The journey was very scenic
Over hills and dales we went.

The fields laid out
       in every shade of green -
good to see new towns and places
       we'd never seen before.

We went to the pier
       to pick up the boat -
and cross to the place
       called Innellen.

It's home for a week of our holiday
In a house on the edge of the sand
Overlooking the stretch of water
We'd sit and watch the ships sail by.

So quiet and the air so fresh
After the noise and pollution of the city
To soak in the sea-fresh air
Feeling the warm sun on your face.

And let your troubles and worries
       just drift away
Across this lovely stretch of water
       while on holiday in Scotland.

In a place called Innellen.

Mary Agnes Pitt

ROSE OF THE SOUTH

The cobbled streets of Rye
are quaint and very old,
with houses that are peerless
and attractive to behold.

The Mermaid Inn has a cellar
built in the twelfth century,
where smugglers brought their booty
from ships on the rolling sea.

John Wesley preached in Pump Street,
and folks all flocked to hear
the words he spoke, which were eloquent,
tho' they fell on many a deaf ear.

The sea has receded from Rye now
but the Rother still runs deep,
and the windmill stands by the river,
and watches the town while it sleeps.

Daf Richards

HOLIDAY MEMORIES OF NORTH AMERICAN FALL NOVEMBER 11TH 1969

Gently the morning's blushing hue
Embraces the lakeside's tranquil blue,
Highlighting the shore and distant forms
As another thanksgiving day dawns.

Some trees bared in reverance stand
Others are decked in finery grand,
In various attires they do appear
To salute the passing of the year.

Some golden, some red, a few in green
Intermingling leaves or showering scene.
The kaleidoscopes of shapes and form
On the mischievous winds are borne.

Swirling confetti colours in festive fling
Free as flying kites without their string,
Dancing confusingly to some caper
Those brittle leaves of flying paper.

Released they float on lake, or in sky
So brief their life, so soon they die.
Yet they replenish another season
Without question or enquiring reason.

Fruits and leaves shed for this aim
Look not for themselves or lay claim.
They serve only the common good
As living testament to the wood.

If only man could do the same
Seek not fortune, fame or name
With more honest standards unfurled,
Perhaps we'd have a better world.

Then distant memories will live again
Remembering verses as well as refrain.

H D Hensman

HOLIDAY

Come, let us take a holiday
Find some secluded, quiet bay,
Go north or south, go east or west, it doesn't matter where,
As long as there's an open sea.
With boats to sail for such as we,
And sea lanes where the wind blows free, and salt spray in the air.

Where thoughts of things we should have done,
And haven't done - can never come,
The worries of the land behind will seem so very far
For we shall hear the seagulls cry,
We'll watch the green foam swirling by,
And lift our faces to the sky - and thank our lucky star.

B W Lawrence

HOLIDAY FROM HELL

Next week I'm on holiday a rather pleasant thought
I've never been on a plane before, in fact I've never been abroad
All this departure lounge, baggage check-ins is all new to me
I usually stay in England and go to Weston-by-the-Sea

We're in the plane now, it was a nervous walk when I stop and take a look
I'm sitting by the wing - the engines loose, I think I'll read a book
'It's just like getting on a bus' that's what my workmates said
But you can get off a bus, just when you like, it's take-off that I dread

Up in the air - the puffy marshmallow clouds float by
You've missed the food, you've been asleep way up in the sky
When you awake, you do with such a jolt, the engines still attached
I must have dreamt it had fallen off or they had had it patched

You've landed in America and it really is a thrill
Until you're told to hold your fire cos your luggage is in Brazil
What are you gonna do, no clothes, no passport and only a little money
Smoke is coming out of your ears whilst others think it's funny

In your hotel room, you sit awaiting the arrival of your luggage
You glance at the holiday brochure, you keep flicking the page
Cos nowhere in this brochure does it mention anything about Brazil
And your lost luggage, you're getting angry but just you wait until

Not every holiday abroad is 100% or even a close second rate
You might take a plane trip again, different destination, different date
A holiday so you can relax and take and do things in a different way
Not stressed out in a hotel room, no clothes, no money, that's no
                                          holiday need I say

They've finally delivered your luggage at long last, now you can go out
Compensation's what you want of that there is no doubt
You only came here for ten days and already a week has past
Next year I'm going to blackpool, I'll make this foreign trip my last.

Leigh Smart

FOOTSTEPS IN THE SAND

Sharp the outlines when first impressed.
Sunk deep into a shifting surface
Each echoing a silent statement
Of another's individuality.
A meandering trail mirrors life's uncertainties
Yet cannot illuminate the pace at which
It was lived or how.
Upon reflection we know where we went wrong
Criticism reaffirms our own vulnerability.
Are we ourselves when faced with such reality.
Blatantly the tide obtrudes upon a
Receptive shoreline
Eroding with uncaring thought
The shapes that were once so safe on compact ground.
As the tide those feet have now journeyed
To another shore.
Better to dream of other beginnings.

Arthur Pugh

HOLIDAY

Met by a vase of flowers, and a pint of milk,
Coastguard Cottage No 1, received.
Across Dartmoor, and North Devon we came,
High on *the tranquillity map,*
Of the Country.

Receiving the key,
From a small family garage,
That still *served,*
We descended the narrow lane,
To the coast.

Hanzel and Grettally in the woods,
Stood the cottage,
Dark and wet in October, but the wood-burning stove,
Soon created a furnace.

You painted a still-life in the sitting-room,
While I explored for autumn leaves,
Speckled and brown,
On the path to the beach.

The large blue rounded, polished rocks,
Stretched out to meet the sea.
Strange, when the cliffs were red.
From that distance,
Clovelly looked like a fishing village still,
And not a guarded factory,
Producing nostalgia-tokens.

The holiday was paid with money,
For my *disability rehousing.*
I still have not many sticks of furniture,
But I remember that sea,
And it's so much healthier.

Steve Taylor

DON'T RELY ON PICTURES

Through doorways down halls in lifts and on stairs,
On buses, in cars, through streets unaware.
Board the train pass the station,
From centre to coast.
Ride the train, feed the donkey,
Do what you like most.
There's Punch and there's Judy,
A kiss me quick hat,
A funfair, a golf course,
I'd like to do that.
Then off to the station to board the last train.
Develop the pictures, you'll go there again.
No time? The years pass and everything changes.
You get there at last, the pictures have faded.
The fair's lost its fun,
Punch has left Judy.
The golf's gone off course,
You can't find a donkey.
So back through the streets and onto the platform,
Board the next train, go back where you came from.
You've wasted your time caught up in your business,
Let life pass you by.
The pictures are witness.

Sue Barlow

CHILDHOOD MEMORIES

Under a cloudless sky
we walked through the wood.
These were happy days,
the summers of my childhood.

In ripe golden meadows
we ran after one another.
I remember being the shadow
of my clever, big brother.

Busy, free holiday time
spent fishing in little brooks,
with a string for a fishing line
and a sort of homemade hooks.

Summers of incandescent fireflies,
chasing for endless hours,
bright coloured butterflies,
flitting from flower to flower.

Yearly, we left the city bustle
for the Tirrenian seaside.
Building tunnels and sandcastles,
waiting for the incoming tide.

Weekend family outings
to the park of the Cascine,
flying the kite shouting,
or splashing in the piscine.

Under the blazing sun
we went picking blackberry.
Blessed, innocent fun
we were young and merry.

Licia Johnston

CORNISH CLIPS

A week in Cornwall, oh what bliss!
Sun, sand, sea and much more.
A visit I try not to miss,
It makes my spirits soar.

Such rugged cliffs and stormy seas,
Long walks along the coast.
The local people aim to please,
Willing to be your host.

Of their roots they're fiercely proud,
Their language and their work
Many catch fish when they're allowed
But regulations lurk!

Cornwall has lots to do and see
Such a popular place
A genuine Cornish cream tea
Puts a smile on your face.

The Minack for dramatic art
Theatre in a rock!
For painting and sculpture where start?
To St Ives Tate we flock.

But art abounds in every form
Where e'er we choose to look
Annual festivals are the norm
And recipes to cook.

Cornwall is steeped in history,
Smugglers and tin mines too
King Arthur, magic, mystery
Daily relived anew.

Sheila Cochrane

ISLANDS APART

Not for me the brash bright Costas
The disco lights, the loud café
My holidays are quiet and tranquil
Off Cornwall's shores not far away.

Islands set in a clear blue sea
The silver sands, the pink sea thrift
The Oyster Catcher calling, calling
From these lovely islands set adrift.

Boats leaving the harbour with time to explore
St Mary's, St Martin's, St Agnes and Gugh
To walk on the seashore and search for the shells
To potter around the little town of Hugh.

Abbey gardens on Tresco, a tropical delight
Bishop Rock lighthouse, rolling waves almost hilly
Walks to the headland, the boat from Penzance
Holidays memories - the lovely Isles of Scilly.

Jean Tester

EVERYBODY LOVES SATURDAY NIGHT

Holiday in Ghana
From suburban Surrey
Groundnut 'chop'
Mangoes and curry
Labadi beach
Surf in the sea
Palm trees bounty
Coconuts for free
Houses on stilts
Verandahs wire-netted
Trees cut back
For snakes to be vetted
Red earth are the anthills
Gigantic and high
Green grows the mould
On clothes left to lie
Bush telegraph drumbeat
Jungle humid with heat
Each Saturday night
Dance to the band
Brandy and ginger
Wasn't life grand

Accra

NO, WE CAN'T TAKE THE FISH

Yes, I know it's still early, it's not even light,
So do try to be quiet and don't start to fight.
Dad likes to go early, avoid all the queues.
Get dressed now, quickly, there's no time to lose.
Take some books, some puzzles and something to munch,
A big flask of coffee and lots of packed lunch.
The surfboard, the football and skates, if you must.
The dog's bed, the basket, the car's fit to bust.
A windbreak? We'll take that, no, we can't take the fish,
The computer, the TV or the satellite dish.
Am I being sarcastic? Yes, I know that's not nice.
No, I really don't think so, no you can't take your mice!
The dog's bowl, some water, an airbed, the kite?
But you never, ever fly it - if it's windy you might.
A deckchair and a sunbed, a needle, some thread.
Of course take your camera, please get out of bed!
Your golf clubs, his fishing rod, their buckets and spades.
The cases, some sunscreen, some cards and my shades,
Tennis racquets and the frisbee, they've all got to go.
Where will you put them? I'm afraid I don't know.
Please try to eat breakfast, no you can't have some grapes.
Yes, we are taking music, I've got all my tapes.
Umbrella? Our raincoats? You think it might rain?
I'm beginning to wish we were going by train.
Just get into the car. It's time we were off.
Yes, I have packed that medicine you need for your cough.
Now be quiet, sit still. Put that box on your lap.
Yes, I'm quite sure I packed it. Now, where is that map?
Loaded to the gunnels, this is supposed to be fun,
Packing for our holiday, just a week in the sun.

Barbara Prager

BAGGABLES
(THANK YOU 'L' AND 'T')

B	Because I sailed on Baggables
A	Around Ionian seas
G	Good dreams come floating back to me:
G	Greek wine with feta cheese,
A	And when the blazing sun went down
B	Behind a towering hill
L	Like Lotus-eaters we relaxed
E	Enchantment with us still.
S	Spellbound - no longer free.
B	Beyond the shores the dolphins came
A	Around the yacht one day -
G	Gliding, diving, playing, leading -
G	Great joy had come our way.
A	And when they left we found a beach
B	Beneath a lowering hill
L	Like Lotus-eaters we relaxed
E	Enchantment with us still.
S	Suborned - we went to sea.
B	Back home at last I sit and think
A	About that magic time.
G	Greek islands calling us to stop,
G	Grand views that were sublime;
A	And when we sipped the Grecian wine
B	Beside a rambling rill
L	Like Lotus-eaters we relaxed
E	Enchantment with us still.
S	So thank you - 'L' and 'T'.

Evelyn Golding

CAROUSEL

Frightening crematorium curtain
Closes off the past for ever,
Totally conceals the future.

So too at airport destination
Carousel screen-drape veils in mystery
What occurred before it was pushed through
By our items of essential baggage -
By we ourselves in fact,
Moving round life's cycle steadily
To the final curtained exit,
Beyond which who can possibly discern
What will or might befall?

Yet surprisingly it all recurs:
(We) our luggage reappears.
Inexorably it re-revolves;
But holdalls, packs, get snatched away,
Or else appallingly do not emerge.

Thus what before had seemed unquestionable,
Logical, following a clear track,
Is after all quite unpredictable,
Not orderly or comprehensible,
As hitherto we had supposed.

Pat Arrowsmith

MARGATE MEMORIES

Each year in Dad's old clapped out car
For holidays in Margate - not that far
Down on the beach we raced, quite fast
To kids the sea looked very vast

The sand between our naked toes
Swimming trunks, our only clothes
Children laughing, having fun
Underneath a summer sun

Punch and Judy, 'Dreamland' too
I'll not forget that sand beach view
The waves that washed our sandy feet
The sticks of rock and candyfloss, sweet

Donkey rides were all the rage
In this perfect summer bygone age
Simple things - nothing to fear
Freedom in this air so clear

Crabs which scurried from the light
Ice cream stalls all painted bright
Rock pools, seaweed, all great fun
Beneath a summer noon day sun

Hard boiled eggs upon the sands
From Mother's old and toil worn hands
She did her best with what she had
Made sure we all thanked dear old Dad

It may not seem that much these days
But money was scarce in many ways
It may have taken all the year round
To save for this, count every pound

A week in lodgings with Mrs Brown
Our yearly escape from a smoke filled town
Looked forward to by everyone
Under the Margate summer sun.

Terry Martin

CRETE

Sun drenched terraces,
Wrapped with vines.
Bazuki music and dancing,
All entwined.

Blistering wood,
On hanging shutters.
Scorched grass.
Cafés, filled by old men's mutters.

Dark eyed women,
White haired men.
Sun-baked children,
Talking of when,
The boats would return,
Carrying the day's catch.
This is the place where dreams can hatch.

Cicadas, singing,
in the night,
the cockerel crows,
at first light.
The village begins once more
With people doing daily chores.

Picking olives from the trees,
Seeking shelter in the breeze,
the blistering heat, has no
mercy upon bare feet.

This is a place I keep,
In my memoir book.
So come on in and take a look.

Bonnie Harris (13)

SAINTS AND OLIVES

I remember the smell of ripeness there
as the oranges dropped from the trees.
Storks circled high above the new ring road,
funded by the EEC.
Above the damp terraces of Monchique
we watched tree frogs in mountain pools
and ate yet more omelette.
Everywhere Agave flowers made forests
of heath and barren rock.
In the villages, dusty churches reminded me
of Morricone with palm trees.
At midday we stood stock still
for the geckos on the their stone pile,
soaking heat up through silent skins.
The winding road was touched with almond blossom
on the way to Salema, where at night
marsh frogs' coarse croaks rang thickly,
between dark hills and ultimate, terrible stars.

Helen Barber

ISRAELI SOLDIER

I see pictures in my mind
of green uniforms
of the Israeli soldier.
So many of them
born to kill.
And it is beyond
my understanding
all I hope for
the world.
Carrying their guns
just like a shoulder bag
Israel.
Where something so important
becomes trivial and
it chills my blood
to see this rank and file
uniformed and uninformed.
Full of patriotic fervour
and blind hatred.
Justifying every killing
for the sake of
A dream, a heritage.
In the name of God!

Vivienne Wood

EVERYBODY SMILES AND SAYS HELLO

Silent stars are looking down on me
Golden moon above the silver sea
Island in the sun you shine so bright
Paradise on earth both day and night

Waterfalls and rivers call my name
My soul lived here long before I came
Island in the sun you shine so bright
Paradise shines through your morning light

Every flower and every tree
Beautiful eternally
There is the place I'll always want to go
Everybody smiles and says hello

Noreen E Kane

THE ABORIGINAL FACE

White bandage gone grey
In the same mouldy way
As the coloured clothes merged
Into the dry red dirt
That stuck to the skin
Of her limping limb.
Her stone black eyes
Were fully disguised
In the black wrinkles that tied
The face she was unable to hide.
Stumbling hopelessly away
The mouth cracked to say
An indistinguishable sound.
Ignoring you don't turn around.
Again this solitary soul
Let out a requesting howl.
Fallen on deaf ears,
She spouts drunken tears
That streak lines of red
Down the path where they're shed,
And still you do not look;
Allow your conscience to be shook.
But I think you do care
And are secretly scared
Of what you don't know,
So you just let her go.
The figure of black mattered hair
Twists away from the hostile stares.
Wobbles, staggers and falls
Against the concrete walls
That imprison her in a world
Where she was helplessly hurled.

The sisters of the earth0
Where forced to give birth
To a lost race
Behind an Aboriginal face.

Eleanor Grourk

FIRST STEPS ABROAD

We'd had Christmas dinner, the pots cleared away,
when up popped the question about a holiday.
I said to the missus let's take a chance
we'll load up the camper and go off to France.

The time it flew by, so feeling happy and merry,
we set off to Poole to catch the ferry.
Safely on board to St Malo we sped,
wondering if we might get down to the Med.

All around France we jovially went,
until that is all our money was spent.
The camper went well it never did shirk,
we arrived back in England to home and to work.

But one thing's for sure, never you fear,
we are going again the same time next year.
So raise up the glass, down with the wine,
you never can tell, we might make the Rhine.

J Spencer

THE AMERICAN DREAM

For many years I longed to visit America so far away across the sea,
  but as I grew older, I felt my chances of achieving my ambition was very
  slim for me.
Then one day my young son Michael said, 'I am thinking of having a holiday
  in the USA,'
  my wife said 'Why don't you go with him' as you can imagine those words
  made my day.
California the sunshine state, to see its beauty was really great.
Beautiful San Diego a West Coast treasure,
  helps to make the American Dream come true at your leisure.
The magic of Hollywood is exciting to see,
  film studios, and Disney World really excited me.
San Francisco is a mecca for tourists with their quaint Cable Cars,
  Fishermans Wharf, and tempting seafood bars.
Trips by boat round San Francisco Bay,
  an interesting visit to Alcatraz, not somewhere where you would like
  to stay.
Twin Peaks overlooking the City, and the Bay,
  the Golden Gate Bridge, very impressive I must say
Arizona is an interesting State,
  to fly over the Grand Canyon in a small plane was exciting, I thought
  it was wonderful, really great.
Yosemite National Park in Central California is a tourist's delight,
  the grandeur of the mountains, the water falls, the wildlife, a fantastic
  sight.
Giant Sequoias, known as Redwoods have stood for centuries straight and
  tall,
  making us insignificant humans feel very humble, and wish we could return
  to see them once more.
This was a holiday I shall always remember,
  when I achieved my ambition and flew to America in the month of
  November.

P G Towner

SOMEWHERE ...

(A holiday romance)

Somewhere I remember you
from days of sun and sand,
I remember how the music played
while we sat hand in hand.

I remember how we drank sweet wine
far into the night,
then walked along a lonely beach
at first touch of morning light.

But somewhere love lost its way
when sunshine turned to rain,
and though I often thought of you
we never met again.

Sometimes I think of you and sigh
remembering the place
where we exchanged our vows of love -
but I can't recall your face.

Ann Rutherford

INFORMATION

We hope you have enjoyed reading this book - and that you will continue to enjoy it in the coming years.

If you like reading and writing poetry drop us a line, or give us a call, and we'll send you a free information pack.

Write to

Arrival Press Information
1-2 Wainman Road
Woodston
Peterborough
PE2 7BU